Oliver's War

Oliver's War

An Adirondack Rebel Battles the Rockefeller Fortune

Lawrence P. Gooley

Lawrence P. Gooley

Bloated Toe Publishing
Peru, New York 12972

Other books by the author:
A History of the Altona Flat Rock
Lyon Mountain: The Tragedy of a Mining Town
Out of the Darkness: In Memory of Lyon Mountain's Iron Men
The Battle of Plattsburgh Question & Answer Book
A History of the Altona Flat Rock – Silver Anniversary Edition

Bloated Toe Publishing, Peru, NY 12972

Library of Congress Catalog Number 2007902867

ISBN: 978-0-9795741-0-8

Copies of this title and the titles listed above may be obtained by writing:
Bloated Toe Enterprises
PO Box 324
Peru, NY 12972

or

Go to Bloated Toe Enterprises website:
URL: www.bloatedtoe.com
email: info@bloatedtoe.com

The cover graphic entitled "Log Cabin in the Mountains" is an original Scratchboard Illustration by Michael Halbert

Printed and bound by
Boyd Printing Company
5 Sand Creek Road
Albany, New York 12205

Manufactured in the United States of America

Contents

Acknowledgments

The author would like to thank the following individuals for their efforts in trying to provide illustrations and/or information. They are:

Linda AuClair, Librarian, Goff-Nelson Memorial Library, Tupper Lake, N.Y.

Michael Burgess, Instructional Support Assistant, Special Collections, Feinberg Library, Plattsburgh State University College (PSUC), Plattsburgh, N.Y.

Timothy and Cheryl Gagne of Chase Mills, N.Y. Tim is the son of Angie Gagne, and grandson of "Black Joe" Peryea of Brandon.

Jean Goddard, Town Historian, Westville, N.Y.

Debra Kimok, Special Collections Librarian, Feinberg Library, Plattsburgh State University College (PSUC), Plattsburgh, N.Y.

Michel Lamoureux of Quebec City, Quebec, Canada. Michel is a genealogist of the Lamoureux family.

David Minnich, Director, Wead Library, Malone, N.Y.

Carol Poole of the Franklin County Historical and Museum Society and House of History, Malone, N.Y.

Gloria Pratt, President of the Northern New York American-Canadian Genealogical Society (NNYACGS), Keeseville Civic Center, Keeseville, N.Y.

Gregory Quenell, Assistant Professor of Mathematics, Plattsburgh State University College (PSUC), Plattsburgh, N.Y. Greg graciously allowed the use of two aerial photographs of Bay Pond.

Neil Surprenant, Director of Educational Resources, Joan Weill Library, Paul Smith's College, Paul Smith's, N.Y.

Loyola Thornton of Tupper Lake, N.Y. Loyola is a sister-in-law of the late Victor Lamora, Oliver Lamora's grandson.

Michele Tucker, Librarian, Saranac Lake Free Library, Saranac Lake, N.Y.

Trina Yeckley, Archivist, the National Archives and Records Administration in New York City.

Special thanks to my partner, Jill McKee, for her excellent work on the illustrations, and for her solid support and advice.

I would also like to acknowledge the invaluable work of the Northern New York Library Network, with headquarters in Potsdam, N.Y. The network has dramatically improved research capabilities, especially in the field of digitization.

Their Northern New York Historical Newspapers database covering Clinton, Essex, Franklin, Jefferson, Lewis, Oswego and St. Lawrence counties is one of the finest public resources in the state.

Introduction

There were a few specific reasons why I chose to tell Oliver Lamora's story. First of all, it is simply a great story. To learn more, I read the brief accounts of Oliver's travails in Alfred Donaldson's wonderful *A History of the Adirondacks*, and in Theodore Chapman White's *Adirondack Country*.

Both are excellent books covering a variety of topics, but in neither of those volumes was Lamora given a fair shake. Stories published in the 1920s were repeated, containing many inaccuracies and omitting many critical details.

For instance, Lamora was described as "a tall and erect old fellow." Actually, at the age of 21, Oliver stood under five feet, five inches tall. Trivial, perhaps, but an example of just one error that has been repeated for more than a century. Other discrepancies of greater significance addressed his motives and actions, vital to defining the truth.

Most important were the details of the battle between Lamora and William Rockefeller, who represented the wealthy landowners. Here the record has never been set straight. Too often Rockefeller was give a free pass by obsequious writers and reporters. There is far more to the story than has ever been related, and it's all here, with no glossing of the facts.

It's important to note that Lamora's adversary was William, the brother of John D. Rockefeller. Many stories have erroneously named William G. (Goodsell) Rockefeller, who was actually William Rockefeller's son. The William Rockefeller who opposed Lamora was in the stratosphere of American business and power.

Often the authors of yesteryear had to rely heavily upon hearsay and tales passed on by word of mouth. Memories of events change as time passes, but today we can access hundreds of newspaper archives and read the stories as they happened. It is a luxury that is yielding some real treasures.

In Lamora's case, we discover an Adirondack classic, a pioneer woodsman who battled to keep the traditional mountain life intact. To some, he might seem a hero. But, hero or not, he had the courage to stand up and fight against fantastic odds.

That was the story of America's birth, and it is the story of our own Oliver Lamora.

1

Prelude to War

In spring 1902, amidst the wilds of far northern New York State, an Adirondack mountain man was charged with trespassing on another man's property. Ordinarily, this would be an incident of little consequence, destined for settlement in a local frontier court.

Instead, this seemingly innocuous event spawned a saga that garnered newspaper headlines from coast to coast, frequently appearing on the front page of the *New York Times* and the *Washington Post*. It was the pauper versus the millionaire, the mountain man versus the sophisticate, the humble woodsman versus the oil tycoon.

It was Oliver Lamora versus William Rockefeller.

At the time, the logging industry was a core component of northern New York's economy. There was no shortage of employment opportunities most of the time, as the discovery of high-grade iron ore across the region in the 1800s resulted in a bonanza for the big lumber companies. Hundreds of thousands of cords of wood were needed each year to feed the charcoal kilns, which in turn fed the furnaces of the iron interests.

For certain, lumber had many uses, and a considerable amount of New England's timber harvest went to the rebuilding of the south after the Civil War. But in far northern New York, for many years it was the iron industry that was the primary force behind the success of the lumber companies. When iron production needs waned, the effects were felt right down through the ranks of the haulers and choppers.

To survive those lean periods of unemployment, men turned more than ever to the woodlands as their basic source of food and other necessities. The abundant, diverse wildlife of the northern forest provided everything a man needed.

Though hunting and fishing were undeniably enjoyable, they were not yet sporting pastimes for mountain residents. They were instead vital components of survival, and from a very young age, boys were taught the skills necessary to become successful hunters and fishermen.

The wild nature of the Adirondacks wasn't popular only with the natives. Vacationers and travelers frequently visited the region, and they liked what they saw. Embellished tales of great hunting and fishing trips in the Adirondack wilds soon surfaced in newspapers, magazines, and books.

Artists and writers of the period also focused substantial efforts on touting the beauties and wonders of nature in New York's scenic northern mountains. Still others marveled at the health-enhancing effects of the pure mountain air.

The charm and beauty of the north woods soon proved irresistible to men and women alike. Around this attraction grew an entire industry. The Adirondacks became a focus of summer recreation, much to the benefit of mountain residents. Clients paid for food, lodging, transportation and a myriad of other services which the natives were more than willing to provide.

Successful outdoorsmen of the mountains provided guiding services to outsiders, and as the Adirondacks surged in notoriety, more and more people came. Locals put up with the behavioral excesses of their often wealthy clients, and in doing so, raised their own standard of living.

Among those visitors to the mountains were the elite of society, the new nobility of a fledgling democracy. These were people with money and power, men who were accustomed to getting what they wanted. As it turned out, they wanted the Adirondacks.

In the mid-1800s, America was developing a line of very wealthy, successful families apart from those with backgrounds in huge farms and tobacco plantations. Some were connected to the utilization of natural resources like oil, iron, and lumber. Others found fortune in transportation, especially railroads, or in the newspaper business.

As their fortunes grew to previously unimaginable proportions, many of these men sought escape from the intensity of the business world. A vacation in the mountains, with the basal pursuits of a man's natural roots in hunting and fishing, was just the ticket, and a popular ticket it was. Politicians, leaders of industry, and even presidents made the Adirondacks their playground of choice.

As America's industries developed, business titans began to funnel their finances into prestigious homes of extreme grandeur, mostly located in fashionable urban neighborhoods. Then, taking a cue from the wealthy elite of Europe, American prosperity began to display itself more and more in grand rural estates during the so-called "Gilded Age," the decades of growth following the Civil War. These estates featured spacious homes built within the confines of expansive, private preserves.

Best known of all from that era is the Biltmore Estate, the brainchild of George W. Vanderbilt II. George was the grandson of Cornelius Vanderbilt, the fabulously wealthy railroad and shipping magnate. The grounds of George's estate spanned 125,000 acres, and the Biltmore mansion today remains the largest private home ever constructed in the United States.

Completed in 1895 after six years of labor, the Biltmore mansion is a 175,000-square-foot representation of the grand châteaux architecture of the Loire Valley in France. During his travels as a leading member of America's "idle rich," George had become enamored of the vast, self-sustaining country estates of Europe. In Biltmore, he brought the concept home to the Blue Ridge Mountains in Asheville, North Carolina.

With his generous inheritance, George Vanderbilt was financially capable of indulging himself in any fashion, and that's exactly what he did at Biltmore. Among his interests was the fairly new concept of active forest management as a method of preservation and perpetuation.

That idea, known as silviculture, fit well with Vanderbilt's plan to make the preserve self-supporting. Instead of just logging the estate grounds indiscriminately, he sought a system of gradual harvest that would provide a continuous income.

To pursue that goal, Vanderbilt hired Gifford Pinchot to oversee the extensive acreage surrounding Biltmore. Pinchot was a well-educated man who had worked at forestry concepts since his youth, having been guided in that direction by his father.

For three years, Pinchot practiced the harvesting of Biltmore's trees as a vital component in his system of forest use and preservation. Among other things, he invoked the concept of sustainable yield, as opposed to the drastic denuding practices of most logging companies.

Under his guidance, lumber sales contributed to the solvency of the Biltmore estate. Pinchot would go on to a great career in forestry, serving as the first Chief of the Forest Service. His ideas of conservation are the basis for many forestry practices to this day.

The mightiest financiers of the Gilded Age – the Carnegies, Goulds, Morgans, Rockefellers, and Vanderbilts – were by nature very competitive men. To demonstrate their great wealth, a decadent game of one-upmanship developed as each family built opulent mansions at great expense.

After George Vanderbilt completed his project in North Carolina, the emphasis shifted to the rural scene. With the Biltmore Estate as the newest benchmark of incredible wealth, other families of great means began to seek their own country manors, modeled generally after the fiefdoms of old Europe. In a land that lacked actual nobility, these men would become America's land barons.

The attention of many of these business moguls was focused on the Adirondack Mountains of New York State. The forbidding nature of the mountains and the difficult weather conditions of the region had left the area sparsely populated and largely undeveloped. Hardy, resourceful woodsmen had managed to extract a living from the land, but survival was dependent upon the many resources provided by nature.

During this same period, America was experiencing phenomenal growth, and lumber was a primary component of that expansion. Much of the lumber supply came from the mountains of the northeastern states. New York's Adirondacks were heavily logged, particularly in the eastern sections. Clear-cutting was common, and many unscrupulous loggers cared nothing about the swath of destruction they left behind.

Visitors who had read tales of the wonderful scenery and spectacular views so prominent in the Adirondack Mountains were sometimes disappointed at what they found. In some areas, especially along the eastern fringes, thousands of acres of forest had been wiped out, creating the look of a desolate wasteland. Concerned citizens began to sound the alarm: the Adirondacks needed to be protected.

Earlier, around the year 1850, the conservation movement in America had begun to make itself known. Various issues were debated for several decades, and the emphasis of the pro-conservation forces was on the outright preservation of valuable resources, including forested land.

There was one very distinct reason for preservation of New York's mountains: a link had been identified between the removal of forests and the failure of natural water systems. A reliable water supply was dependent upon a healthy, standing forest. As Biltmore's manager put it:

> The connection between forests and rivers is like
> that between father and son. No forests, no rivers.
> So a forester may not be wholly beyond his depth
> when he talks about streams. - Gifford Pinchot

It was a fact of life that watersheds supported all industries and enterprises of man. Of great importance was the discovery that a watershed rendered devoid of tree cover soon lost its ability to retain moisture, leading to intense erosion and ultimate failure of the water system.

When politicians and businessmen began to face those realities of science, the voices of conservation were heard.

Among other things, it was feared that depletion of the Adirondack forests would reduce the capacity of the water sources that supplied the state canal system. When commerce was threatened, lawmakers and industrialists took notice.

Another growing issue in the Adirondacks was accessibility. Even in the 1880s, the posting of private holdings, especially large tracts, was becoming a problem. J.B. Harrison, the Secretary of the American Forestry Congress, noted in 1889 that two such blocks of land restricted access to nearly 90,000 acres.

Said Harrison: "Visitors to the Adirondacks seeking health or pleasure may as well take down their maps and mark this region of their unrestrained wandering and delight, 'No Trespassing Here!'"

Conservationists, loggers, sportsmen, and mountain residents all had varying opinions and interests to be considered in determining the future of the Adirondacks. Another faction, wealthy businessmen, would prove to be perhaps the most influential force of all. Their combined efforts and great resources gave them a voice that was heard above all others.

In early 1890, in a little-publicized meeting, many of these wealthy business leaders convened in New York City to unite for a common cause: "The prevention of further destruction of the Adirondacks by lumbermen, and the establishment of a State Forest Park in that region." They formally organized as the Adirondack Park Association (no connection to modern groups).

The gathering listened as Dr. Alfred Loomis pleaded for protection of the great forest, which had been proven to be literally life-saving to many people suffering from previously incurable pulmonary diseases like tuberculosis. Simply resting and breathing the air among the evergreens had saved countless lives, and spawned an entire industry in the Saranac Lake region.

Loomis pointed out that this curative effect had been widely used for the past two decades, but would soon end at the hands of the railroads and lumbermen unless the state stepped in to save the forests.

Among the group of politicians and businessmen Loomis addressed were a number of men who had made their fortunes in railroads and lumber operations. Many of them were, in part, responsible for the very destruction that Loomis was seeking to halt.

Other speakers followed Loomis, detailing the devastation in the Adirondacks, and gauging the future. It was suggested that the state should control the forests, which were vital to the public's interests.

It was also noted that the state could formulate a plan to utilize the forests, employing conservation methods while reaping revenues that would be used to further develop and protect the forest preserve.

The room was filled with men of power and great financial means. They sat, they listened, and they heard more than would the average citizen. The shrewd business acumen of those men of the Gilded Age revealed a golden opportunity before them.

Already familiar with the vast forested wilderness, the voluminous wildlife, and the great potential of the Adirondacks as a vacation destination, these men saw more. Much more.

This new Adirondack Park Association was led by a finance committee of some repute, including J.P. Morgan, William C. Whitney, and John D. Rockefeller. Perusing the minutes of the meeting, a *New York Times* correspondent noted with skepticism, "Some things are queer, and not the least of queer things is to see a St. Lawrence lawyer and a lot of politicians tumbling over one another in the effort to save the Adirondacks. What's up?"

That comment would prove to be remarkably prophetic.

These men were keenly aware that millions of acres of forested land were coveted by the State of New York, but that state coffers were limited. Men of that ilk were always looking for more power and more profit, and the Adirondacks offered great potential in both respects if privately owned.

Most of the participants at the meeting had already experienced the pleasures offered by the mountains, having rented or purchased camps there and enjoyed some of the best hunting and fishing in the country. Here before them was an impressive opportunity for great prestige, profit, and pleasure.

In the same vein as Vanderbilt's efforts in North Carolina at Biltmore, many of them had already purchased Adirondack land and were developing their own estates. Now, fully aware of the potential value of the vast timberlands they possessed, several of these titans of industry began to accumulate other large tracts of land within New York's northern mountains.

In the meantime, the thirst for profit had driven many logging companies to continue clear-cutting the land. Conservationists pushed their message unremittingly, and public outcry over the depredation of the Adirondack forest was finally heard by state lawmakers.

In 1890, Governor David Hill asked the New York State legislature to create an Adirondack Park that would eventually be absorbed into the forest preserve, thereby offering lasting protection to the woodlands and the valuable watershed.

In 1892, newly elected Governor Roswell Flower signed the legislation that created the Adirondack Park. But in 1893, Flower proposed a bill that allowed the Forest Commission to sell timber from the forest preserve, effectively entering the state into the lumbering business, and clouding the concept of a preserve for the people of the state.

The public was irate, and reaction eventually led to the "Forever Wild" amendment that passed the legislature in 1894, taking effect on January 1, 1895. This one short clause stated it clearly:

> The lands of the state, now owned or hereafter acquired, constituting the forest preserve as now fixed by law, shall be forever kept as wild forest lands. They shall not be leased, sold or exchanged, or be taken by any corporation, public or private, nor shall the timber thereon be sold, removed or destroyed.

Alarmingly, the vast acreage of private land within the established park was not bound by the new law, and those private tracts were lumbered intensely between 1890 and 1910.

Still, with a conservation plan in place, it appeared that much of the Adirondack forest was now safe from loggers and greedy capitalists. This would be a park for the people of New York to enjoy through hunting, fishing, and all manner of outdoor pursuits.

Or so it seemed.

It was now state policy to actively seek land for addition to the forest preserve. Money was appropriated by the legislature for the purpose of increasing landholdings within the Blue Line. (The Blue Line was a line of blue ink drawn on a map, showing the new park's perimeter.)

State land outside of the Blue Line was offered for sale, and the proceeds were then used to purchase land within the Adirondack Park. The state's only competition for this land was men of great financial means, and it is no coincidence that the purchases by private owners accelerated through the 1890s.

The financial resources of America's richest men were far greater than those of the State Forest Commission, and incredibly huge tracts of prime forest lands became the property of private owners. So much for the concept of a public park.

Once the land was in their hands, these men had several inviting options. They could keep the land for themselves and continue to develop exclusive private estates. They could raise the price of the land and offer it for sale to the state for inclusion in the forest preserve, while keeping a portion of it for a smaller estate.

They could also sell the timber first, and then sell the land to the state at a profit. It was noted suspiciously by state officials that each time money was appropriated for more land purchases inside the Blue Line, the selling price of the land suddenly increased. In fact, that was one of the reasons given by the state in 1902 when land purchases were suspended for two years.

Most of the time, when these financial tycoons acquired large tracts of Adirondack woodlands, it was done quietly through purchasing agents. Generally, the details of the transactions were not made public until after the purchases were completed.

Lawyers from area cities like Glens Falls, Plattsburgh, Malone, and Watertown were enlisted to secure many properties, protecting the identities of the buyers.

In this manner, hundreds of thousands of acres of prime Adirondack woodlands were added to the property holdings of some of the country's wealthiest citizens, even as the state expressed interest in those very same properties.

The new owners claimed they were actually providing a service that coincided with the state's plan to preserve the forests and protect the land from further abuse and development.

They proclaimed themselves as "good stewards of the land," even as they posted their properties against all trespassers. In effect, they bought huge tracts of land to keep the forests *from* public use, not *for* public use.

This was not at all attuned to the state's original concept of an open park. To the average citizen, such deals appeared to be driven by nothing but greed. But greed was a mild affront compared to what was to come.

Vast tracts of land with the best hunting and fishing opportunities in the northeast had supported the lifestyle of thousands of New Yorkers living in and around the park lands. That lifestyle was now threatened by the sale of huge chunks of Adirondack acreage.

When wealthy landowners posted their land, they directly affected the lives of locals, depriving them of traditional sources of food and recreation. In the far north, hunting, fishing, picking berries, building homes, and cutting firewood were often necessities of life, and all were dependent on the availability of forested land.

For the wealthy, those were simply activities to be played at while on vacation, the recreational benefits of owning land. What was quaint to them was absolutely vital to many mountain natives, some of whom had lived there for generations.

Adding to the problem for locals was that much of the public land in the nearly 700,000 acre Adirondack Forest Preserve had already been logged. Companies frequently stripped away all valuable timber, and then simply stopped paying taxes on their land, which reverted to the property of the state. If the state sold it, the dollar value was obviously severely reduced.

If the land was added to the forest preserve, it became available to the public, but those thousands of acres, now reduced to stumps and thick brush, offered little in the way of hunting and fishing for farmers and woodsmen.

With much of the public land ravaged, and vast acreage held

in private hands, mountain residents were further restricted. Their very way of life was now hanging in the balance between northern living traditions and the power of the wealthy, who frequently sealed off their private holdings.

The rising value of timber contributed further to the problem of the diminishing forests. Landowners of forested property found themselves sitting on a proverbial gold mine. Advances in the papermaking process, driven by a shortage of clothing rags that were once used to produce pulp, triggered an explosion in the wood-pulp industry in the late 1800s. The monetary value of forested lands skyrocketed.

The appetite for wood pulp was nearly insatiable, and the Adirondacks held a supply that was viewed (wrongly) by some as inexhaustible. Wealthy railroad men pushed their lines deeper and deeper into the wilderness in pursuit of greater lumber profits. Nearly any tree could be used for the different grades of pulp, so all types of woodland held real value.

Locals benefited from the increased availability of work through these lumber operations, but the long-range ramifications were detrimental to their future, removing the very resources that they counted on for daily life.

Along with the railroads penetrating into the depths of New York's wilderness came depletion of the forest, despoilment of many pristine areas, and a drastic increase in forest fires.

When forestry officials mapped the fire situation, they noted that forest fires frequently followed the paths of the rails. It was believed that sparks and cinders from passing trains were causing many of the fires. Sometimes hundreds of thousands of acres of woodlands went up in smoke in a single season.

With such important issues at stake, many different interests were battling for supremacy in the Adirondacks. As politicians, lumbermen, sportsmen, nature-lovers, conservationists, and mountain residents persuasively voiced their ideas, big money stepped in and changed the face of the northern forests. The effects of those changes are still clearly evident more than one hundred years later.

The big money came from the wealthiest men in the country. Many of the most prosperous families in America had already established a presence in the Adirondacks through ownership of what became known as "Great Camps," elaborate, luxurious enclaves created in the wilderness. The camps were often accepted as environmentally friendly since local materials were used for most of the structures.

Only those built in the architectural style created by William West Durant were called Great Camps. These were lavish estates furnished in luxury, having little in common with the traditional Adirondack camp experience. Some camps had more buildings than entire Adirondack villages.

The Great Camps and other grand estates were elaborate in design, and the surrounding grounds often stretched for miles in all directions. Maintenance needs of these estates led to the employment of local residents, which was viewed as a real benefit.

Not all wealthy Adirondack landowners built Great Camps on their properties. Some built castles, or mansions, or elaborate homes of their own design. Again, it wasn't the presence of the lavish homes that impacted the residents of the mountains. It was the closing of the vast estates surrounding the homes that caused alarm, and served to antagonize locals.

Some owners even banned employees from hunting, fishing, or walking on their land for any reason other than job-related. The posting of huge expanses of land, even in an area with millions of acres, resulted in resentment among homelanders whose families had survived there for generations, freely roaming the wilds. For many of them, life would never be the same.

Hundreds of people of varying levels of wealth owned or rented camps in the Adirondacks, or stayed at luxurious hotels during the warmer months. They ranged from moderately successful businessmen to America's (and the world's) richest families – the Carnegies, Morgans, and Vanderbilts.

Head and shoulders above those families stood the Rockefeller brothers, John D. and William. In the second half of the nineteenth century, they built a financial empire that made them the most powerful businessmen in America, and the richest to boot. The incredibly far-reaching tentacles of their Standard Oil Trust had made them two of the world's richest men.

As the outright leader of Standard Oil, John D. was sometimes referred to as the most hated man in America. William, playing only a slightly lesser role, was one of the most powerful, feared businessmen in the country.

J.D. and William had long been familiar with the allure of the Adirondacks. Famed and beloved hotelier Paul Smith had frequently played host to the Rockefeller brothers over the years, guiding them on fishing and hunting expeditions. J.D.'s daughter and son-in-law owned a camp on one of Smith's lakes, and the oil titans were regular visitors.

J.D. and William both developed an interest in establishing a presence in the Adirondacks, and like everything the Rockefellers had done previously, it would be on a grand scale.

While J.D. considered building a large camp near his daughter, William had plans for an Adirondack getaway more in keeping with Vanderbilt's efforts at Biltmore. He hoped to create an expansive private park, while reaping profits from lumbering at various locations on the preserve.

The popularity of private parks in America was on the rise. In an article praising such estates owned by millionaires, the *Fort Wayne*

How did tourists discover the Adirondacks a century ago? Advertising columns like the one above from the *New York Times* appeared regularly in newspapers across the state.

(Indiana) *News* unwittingly revealed one of the main points of contention regarding the park phenomenon: "Today there are millions of acres set aside for this purpose, in order that the game may be properly protected from the pot hunter and kept for the true sportsman."

That issue, the pot hunter versus the true sportsman, was especially applicable to the Adirondacks, and would become a major issue. Hunting to kill and eat your prey was considered bourgeois by the wealthy, as opposed to the more noble aim of hunting to hang a trophy on the wall.

Despite his status as a newcomer to the Adirondacks, William Rockefeller was no stranger to estate ownership. He already owned a preserve in Connecticut, and he and brother John were neighbors in Tarrytown, New York, where William lived in a spectacular turreted castle.

Together, their adjacent estates covered 1,200 acres. Both men continued to expand their holdings by aggressively pursuing land purchases from locals.

In comparison to his Tarrytown site, William's plans for the Adirondacks were far more ambitious. Just to the north of Paul Smith's vast property was a huge forest, much of it still wild.

With the vision of a ruthless, powerful businessman whose reach knew no bounds, William Rockefeller set about creating his own private kingdom, using the same coercive tactics that he and his brother used to build the most dominant business organization in the world.

As usual, he did this through an anonymous agent, in this instance Attorney John P. Kellas of Malone, New York, a small city about thirty miles northeast of the proposed park site. Kellas worked at acquiring thousands of acres of property on Rockefeller's behalf.

Most of America's wealthiest tycoons had purchased camps in the Adirondacks further to the south, mainly between Raquette Lake and the Saranac Lakes. In the northernmost fringes of the Adirondack Park, where Rockefeller's interests lay, there were far fewer individual owners. Vast amounts of acreage were still in the hands of lumbering interests.

As one of the world's richest men, William Rockefeller

certainly had the financial capabilities of meeting anyone's asking price. Historically, though, he and his brother had always driven a hard bargain, rarely paying more than what they felt was fair value for any property.

The land that William sought was mostly wilderness two decades earlier, when, in the mid-1870s, a young naturalist named Theodore Roosevelt visited the area several times during a multi-year nature study.

Roosevelt and partner Henry D. Minot noted the Hudsonian Chickadee "in small flocks at Bay Pond" in their four-page pamphlet entitled *The Summer Birds of the Adirondacks in Franklin County, N.Y.*

Bay Pond was one of the most notable bodies of water within the huge, sparsely populated region north of the St. Regis Lakes. Scattered about the vicinity were many lumber camps that had been built up over the years. A few had grown into small hamlets, and some, like Derrick, even had their own post office.

The largest settlement in the territory was known as Brandon, located about seven miles slightly northwest of Paul Smith's hotel, and only a few miles northeast of Bay Pond.

Unlike the nearby villages of St. Regis Falls and Santa Clara several miles north, Brandon was fully within the confines of Rockefeller's intended purchase site.

2

Brandon Comes to Life

Brandon village had really only begun to thrive barely a decade before William Rockefeller's arrival. Loggers had worked the area sporadically in the post-Civil War years, but in the early 1880s, dramatic changes began when a pair of wealthy lumbermen from Muskegon, Michigan, Patrick Ahearn Ducey and John Torrent, expanded their business into New York's north woods.

In early 1882 it was reported that Ducey and Torrent had paid $130,000 for more than 17,000 acres in the towns of Waverly and Brandon in Franklin County. While developing plans for lumber camps and mills on their new holdings, they also pursued other nearby tracts of timber.

After a prolonged court battle with Samuel F. Vilas, a wealthy landowner from Plattsburgh in neighboring Clinton County, Ducey and Torrent succeeded in securing another 25,000 acres for the princely sum of $260,000. (This was no small deal. In 2005, the total price for the 42,000 acres translated to approximately $7.5 million.)

Another man, John Hurd, was also making his mark in this same general area. Hurd was primarily a railroad man, and with financing from a pair of partners, he began laying tracks into the northern forest to serve the needs of the logging companies and their lumber mills. Until that time, there was no modern, efficient system for getting the lumberman's product to market from this remote area.

Hurd's Northern Adirondack Railroad completed a line from Moira south to St. Regis Falls in late September 1883. The terrain was extremely rough across the region, prompting this prescient description by a Canton reporter:

> Nearly the entire region is ill-fitted for agricultural purposes, owing to the barrenness of soil and the high altitude. The places that spring up while lumbering lasts will decline in the near future, like other places where the timber is exhausted.
>
> As the company can purchase no more forest lands from the state, their operations are limited to a few years.

In 1885, Hurd was extending the rail line to reach Santa Clara, another very active logging site. Once at Santa Clara, plans were made to reach further south into the wilderness. Stations were proposed for Spring Cove and Madawaska, with the end-of-the-line stop intended near Buck Mountain, thirteen miles south of Santa Clara.

The final stop on Hurd's line would be known as Buck Mountain, or Paul Smith Station, in the heart of the wilderness. In addition to the income from loggers, Hurd would gain revenue from passengers riding the rails to Paul Smith Station in order to access the general Saranac Lakes area.

With such grand plans, Hurd needed financing to the tune of $300,000, which he raised at the price of $100 per share. As further incentive to potential investors, the plan had been upgraded to run an additional line from Paul Smith Station all the way to Tupper Lake (known as Faust at that time, or Tupper's Lake). The rails would run southeast through the Bay Pond area, accessing many additional tracts of timber.

In June 1886 tracks were being laid south of Santa Clara by the newly formed Northern Adirondack Extension Railroad. Several miles south, where the Ducey and Hurd properties met, was the site chosen for Paul Smith Station.

There, 160 lots were defined in preparation for the village that would soon take shape. Besides the general street layout, plans were made for home building sites, stores, hotels, and a variety of businesses, including a very large lumber mill.

The rail line reached Paul Smith Station in July, opening great new possibilities for the area. Visitors to the mountains could now leave New York City and travel in comfort north to Rouses Point, west to Moira, and south to Paul Smith Station without ever having to change rail cars.

From there, it was a one-hour ride by stagecoach to nearby hotels. The entire journey took about nineteen hours, and, as of July 9, 1886, that route joined the daily offerings of northern rail service.

The new railroad was carrying the trade from three or four smaller mills located near the tracks in addition to the lumber from Ducey's operations and Hurd's own holdings. Paul Smith Station was suddenly one of the busiest places in the northern Adirondacks.

In July it was decided that the new village would be renamed Brandon, and in mid-November, the site featured the area's newest post office, with Harrison G. Baker as postmaster. The official application for the Brandon Post Office cited a village population of "about 300," and indicated that "probably 500" customers would be served.

In 1887, Brandon was occasionally referred to as Buck Mountain, and the title of Paul Smith Station was still used, especially in literature advertising the services of railroads and hotels. Brandon gradually became the village's accepted name, while Paul Smith Station referred to the actual railroad stop.

Brandon was undergoing the "boomtown" growth so often associated with burgeoning industries. Within a year, the tiny logging camp had become a village bustling with a bakery, a creamery, hotels, and a nearby sporting camp at Bay Pond, complete with guide service and hunting dogs. Dozens of new buildings were under construction, including apartment houses for the mill workers and woodsmen.

The centerpiece of it all was the huge sawmill. John Torrent had sold his interests to George and John Backus, and the firm managing the mill was known as Ducey & Backus. By any standards it was a large operation, one of the most prolific in the entire state.

With a great number of children in school at Brandon, medical care was a growing concern. Exacerbating that need was the high injury rate suffered by mill workers and loggers. A local justice convinced Dr. Charles Haynes of Redford, New York, to come to Brandon and open a practice there.

When Dr. Haynes moved, it sparked a mini-exodus from his former location. The famed Redford Glass Company was by then a thing of the past, and the only hope on the horizon was the developing iron industry. Many Redford residents decided it was far better to move to Brandon and join in the prosperity there. This added substantially to Brandon's population, and there was plenty of work to keep the newcomers busy.

Barely a year old, the new village played host to some very impressive company in summer 1887. President Grover Cleveland and his wife descended from the train at Brandon en route to Saranac Lake, where they planned to celebrate their first wedding anniversary in Adirondack solitude.

Cleveland was the first of many celebrities to take advantage

The Brandon Hotel (1890)

of the convenient northern route into the mountains. With the new travel arrangements available from major metropolitan areas, many of the wealthiest families in America passed through Brandon on their way to the Saranac Lakes region.

For the next few years, Brandon's growth continued at a steady pace, and the population reached around 1,200. There were churches, ladies aid societies, social groups, a school, a barbershop, a drugstore, a blacksmith shop, and all the other services necessary for a thriving village.

In June 1888 Hurd began laying tracks from Brandon south towards Bay Pond, and in 1889, the tracks reached Tupper Lake, a significant accomplishment. This opened Hurd's rail line to more freight business and tourism, and connected his three large mills at Santa Clara, Tupper Lake, and St. Regis Falls.

In 1890, with the work of the Northern Adirondack Extension Railroad completed, that company was absorbed into Hurd's own Northern Adirondack Railroad.

The growth of several lumber towns along the St. Regis River was at times phenomenal, tied directly to the fortunes of Hurd's railroads and the area logging interests, which were led by Ducey and Hurd's companies. In the space of just six years, St. Regis Falls had grown from one hundred to twelve hundred residents.

Santa Clara and Brandon had risen from small logging camps to full-fledged villages, still experiencing growth and expansion. Much of this was related to the latest technology used by Ducey, whose men employed the practice of sawing logs instead of chopping. Mills that had produced a few million feet of lumber per year were now regularly yielding fifteen to twenty million feet.

While the villages prospered, the effects on the great northern forest were catastrophic. In most instances, conservation methods were ignored. Once an area had been cleared of valuable timber, a new line of rails was extended through the devastation to reach other stands deeper into the woods.

Piecemeal logging had already extracted a toll over the past several decades, but now the pace of the destruction was accelerated.

While the outcry by conservationists and preservationists had focused on the condition of the lands of the State Forest Preserve, logging on the fringes of the Adirondacks had continued unabated. Now, as railroads opened up the north to more visitors and tourists, the grim reality became apparent, and the voices of protest increased.

Area residents and employees of the logging companies yielded great benefits from the steady work, as did the companies themselves, but it was fast becoming apparent that they had mortgaged the future. New forestry practices were coming into use, but for the vast virgin forests of the northeastern Adirondacks, it was too late.

A touring reporter, passing through the St. Regis Falls area in 1886, shared this firsthand account of the desolation:

> From here the railroad ascends through what may properly be called a 'slash,' the best of the timber having been taken off years ago, so that now the country on either side of the road, until 'Santa Clare' is reached, presents a dismal array of old trees, lying and standing, among rocks and sandbanks, on hills and in swamps, relieved by a small river, which is filled with millions of feet of spruce logs.

Depletion of the woodlands served the needs of progress, but those centuries-old stands of giant timber were doomed to become a memory. The forest would live on, but only as a shadow of its former self.

Among the men logging in the northern area, Patrick Ducey was the most experienced. Just as mining companies established company towns to work ore deposits, Ducey retained ownership and control of most of his holdings, building homes so that his workers could rent from him. When the timber supply was exhausted, he could move on, and so could the workers he had hired, since most of them didn't own land.

That was Brandon's story in a nutshell. Store operators and residents were discouraged by Ducey from purchasing the land where their buildings stood. When the town was booming, it seemed logical to buy. But Ducey knew that when he pulled up stakes and closed the mill, there would be no employment. None of the land near Brandon was suitable for farming, so most people would be forced to leave the area.

However, the village of Brandon was thriving at the time, and there were still other logging operations in the area. And, the presence of Paul Smith Station kept Brandon connected with the world by rail, allowing for easy access by businessmen and tourists. There did appear to be some advantages to owning property in the village.

John Hurd, the other major player in Brandon's future, was still planning to expand his railroad on a southerly route through the Adirondacks. But, shortly after 1890, things began to turn sour for Hurd. In 1892, he sold the huge mill at Tupper Lake, said at the time to be the largest in New York State.

He soon experienced difficulties with the Northern Adirondack Railroad as well, and in December 1894 Hurd was voted out as president. He repurchased the Tupper mill, but lawsuits exacerbated his problems. Soon there was little left to keep Hurd active in either the railroad or the logging business in northern New York.

The same was true of Ducey. He had come to the northeast with a plan to purchase great tracts of land, develop the timber resources, and move on when he had accomplished his goals. Now, after a decade of logging, his work in the Brandon area was finished.

Though his departure was imminent, Ducey expected to maintain ownership of about 25,000 acres. In perhaps fifteen years, he would return to the site and harvest the new growth of pulp for more profit. By that time, some of the hardwood left standing would also be large enough to yield a nice return.

During Brandon's busiest years as a logging center, Patrick Ducey had cautioned village residents that the area would be deserted once he moved on. As one of the area settlements most dependent on the fortunes of Ducey and Hurd, Brandon's future had always been in question.

Into the 1890s, despite Ducey's warnings, locals persisted in their efforts to purchase property, and he finally acceded to their demands. Many felt that theirs was a village like any other across the region, and life would go on after Ducey departed.

In all, about half of the community purchased their lots and planned to remain, despite a very uncertain outlook. Ducey retained ownership of the rest of the village.

It didn't take long for the changes to begin. After the 1895 lumber season, the big mill at Brandon operated less and less, leaving hundreds of workers frequently unemployed. Just as quickly as the town had sprung up, it was now dismantling, piece by piece.

The mill finally stopped operating in September 1896, putting hundreds of men out of work. A month later, portions of the building itself were being disposed of, and it appeared that the end of Brandon was in sight.

Six months later, Patrick Ducey sold his entire machine shop to Ambrose J. Norton, a businessman with many interests in St. Regis Falls. Within a few weeks, Norton planned to have the complete workings moved to that prospering village seventeen miles northwest of Brandon.

The machine shop was a vital component to the success of any lumber mill. Now that it was gone, reality began to settle in. Ducey's prediction had come true. As he gradually shut down his operations, there was little left to justify the existence of Brandon village.

As time passed and the situation assumed an aura of desperation, a number of families decided to move on. Still, many residents chose to stay and see what the future held.

Hope was ignited when it was reported that Ducey had offered his holdings to Paul Smith. Smith seemed a likely candidate to make the purchase, as he already owned thousands of acres along the southern border of Ducey's land.

But Smith passed on the deal, much to the dismay of the folks of Brandon. At least now Ducey was considering selling his land instead of holding onto it for future harvests. Brandon village might well benefit if a new owner decided to take over.

Little did they know that a financial titan was eyeing the proceedings with great interest.

3

Rockefeller Moves In

In summer 1898 came news that would determine the future of Brandon village. A very significant offer had been made, and Ducey had sold the remainder of his land to one of the world's richest men, William Rockefeller.

Suddenly, Brandon's prospects brightened considerably. The possibilities now seemed endless. John Hurd and Patrick Ducey had done well by the people of Brandon, Santa Clara, and St. Regis Falls, but their combined assets were a pittance compared to the Rockefeller fortune. Here now was real hope, the chance for a renewal of the town's earlier success.

When the purchase was announced in August 1898, Rockefeller was a guest at one of Paul Smith's cottages several miles south of Brandon. In a life of excess and performing on a grand scale, his move to the Adirondacks would be no different. For $50,000, William Rockefeller now owned more than 25,000 acres of mountain forest.

The entire tract of land had been in the hands of Ducey, the last of his timber properties north of Paul Smith's. Along with several mountains and ponds, the purchase included Ducey's mill and about half of the village of Brandon. Residents waited anxiously to see what the future might bring.

They didn't have to wait long. It was abruptly announced

that Rockefeller's property would be incorporated into a private game preserve. In effect, it was a proclamation that Brandon's logging history was just that: history.

The fact that Rockefeller had declared his land a private game preserve wasn't unusual, but it *was* alarming. It followed a trend that had been escalating in recent years. New York State law allowed private landowners to dedicate their properties for the betterment of wild game.

To do so required a published declaration of that intent every week for three consecutive months, along with posting of the property's perimeter with No Trespassing signs. Once those simple criteria were met, the land was considered a private park.

Obviously, this was a law for the wealthy, since no poor people owned large tracts of land. Now, the statute's most controversial clause came into play.

By order, all fish, birds, and other game within the private preserve effectively became the property of the landowner.

Instead of constraining the power of the wealthy landowners, the law allowed them free reign over their forest domains. It was a law that was easily and

Private Park

Whereas, I, William Rockefeller, of the Borough of Manhattan, in the city of New York and state of New York, owning and having the exclusive right to shoot, hunt, and fish on the lands hereinafter described and the waters thereof and thereon, and desiring to devote such lands and waters to the propagation and protection of fish, birds, and game, according to the statute in such case made and provided ... said lands and waters situated, lying, and being in the county of Franklin and State of New York, and in the town of Santa Clara, in said county, desire to and do hereby lay out, devote, and declare all of said lands and waters so owned by me will be used as and for a private park for the purpose of propagating and protecting fish, birds, and game.

An excerpt from one of William Rockefeller's declarations designating his property as a private park frequently abused.

Public tax money was appropriated each year to aid and increase the population of game animals in the Adirondacks, and to support fish hatcheries. Should any of those stocked animals or fish move inside the boundaries of a private game preserve, they were no longer accessible to the public, and for all intents and purposes, were now private property. In effect, state tax monies were providing sport for the wealthy.

Until that law became widely known, it hadn't presented much of a problem. Some wealthy camp owners on smaller lots in the Adirondacks availed themselves of the provisions, but it was only when large tracts of land were cut off from the public that there was widespread consternation.

In many instances, the forest provided the necessities of life. In fact, many laws protecting homesteading once depended upon it. Persons so inclined had been allowed and encouraged by law to settle within places like the Adirondack wilderness.

After a period of time, the property they had nurtured for years became their own. Fish, game, plants, water, and trees were all basic components of survival for the settlers. To cut those necessities off in the Adirondacks was to sever the lifeline of the north.

A typical example of the shock value of private preserves occurred near Brandon a decade earlier in 1889. An alliance of ten lumber companies and private owners announced they were consolidating their lands into one vast, private preserve. Life in the north would never be the same.

Where the public had roamed freely for the past few generations, they were now banned from even setting foot within the private park's boundaries without obtaining special permission. This was a "park" like none other, encompassing more than 250 square miles across Franklin and St. Lawrence Counties.

A few park owners near Brandon, like the St. Regis Paper Company, used a permit system to open their properties to hunters and fishermen. Of course, that made for better relations with the public, and it can be argued that public opinion was the real reason behind the move by St. Regis.

At the time, the company was feeding its gigantic pulp mill operations in Watertown. Previous lumbering by Ducey and others typically left standing any growth below twelve inches in diameter. For the purposes of pulp, most spruce and poplar above the size of a sapling were sufficient, and clear-cutting by St. Regis and others was destroying the forest. Allowing access to sportsmen was a conciliatory gesture.

On the plus side for hunters and fishermen, the St. Regis outfit was one of the few who allowed their land to be used by locals. Most park owners didn't.

The declaration by William Rockefeller establishing a private preserve actually followed a developing trend. At the time of Rockefeller's purchase of the Ducey Tract in 1898, several other landowners in the vicinity of Brandon had already veiled their properties under the private park law.

During the six years previous, thousands upon thousands of acres had been preserved under the names of the Adirondack Land Company, the Everton Gun Club Preserve, O.L. Hinds, the Santa Clara Gun Club, the Waverly Gun Club, and William H. Russell.

A free romp in the woods to hunt and fish was fast becoming a rarity, and Rockefeller was now adding substantially to the problem. Signs warning of No Trespassing began showing up in the vicinity of Brandon village.

But there was also an upside to the situation. To operate a preserve of that scope required the services of many employees. The people of Brandon were prepared to fill those roles and perhaps retain their homes in the bargain. But first, they would have to learn more about the wealthy man's intentions.

By December 1898, Rockefeller had revealed his plans to construct an elaborate estate of thirteen buildings about three miles southwest of Brandon, at Bay Pond. Much of the manpower needed would likely be supplied by local workers. Considering the employment situation at Brandon, this was great news.

Wasting no time, Rockefeller hired supervisors and foremen to handle the construction duties. Even as work progressed on the layout of the estate buildings at Bay Pond, Attorney John Kellas was finalizing the terms of a second land purchase in

Rockefeller's name.

In May 1899, Brandon residents were stunned to learn that the Vilas Tract, approximately 17,000 acres, had been added to Rockefeller's preserve. This increased the Standard Oil titan's holdings in the area to more than 42,000 acres. His property now extended nearly six miles west of the village, and more than seven miles southwest.

The announcement was of great concern in Brandon, and many in the village could read the proverbial writing on the wall. With all of the surrounding lands ensconced in preserves, there would be little opportunity left to earn a living. They were being hemmed in on all sides, and were hardly able to step outside of their own homes without trespassing. In the north woods, this was akin to being held prisoner.

Just a month later, Rockefeller's purchasing agent announced a third land deal, this time securing the Debar Mountain tract several miles northeast of Brandon.

Located between Rockefeller's first purchase (the Ducey land) and this latest acquisition (Debar) stood the Meacham Lake tract, which now divided Rockefeller's properties.

Since the new section purchased was not adjacent to Rockefeller's current holdings at Bay Pond, it was not yet declared a private preserve. The tract included approximately 12,000 forested acres spanning from the Sable Mountains to the slopes of Debar Mountain.

On the heels of the announcement of the Vilas purchase came word of another blockbuster deal in the making. The Meacham Lake tract was being eyed anxiously by Rockefeller, along with one of the best-known of all Adirondack resorts, the Paul Smith property on the St. Regis Lakes, south of Brandon.

Interestingly, if William did purchase Paul Smith's property, he might well become the landlord of his older brother, John D. Rockefeller, the world's richest man. J.D. had recently announced plans to construct a $150,000 "cottage" on the shores of one of Smith's lakes, a place that had become his favorite summer getaway.

As each land deal was announced, speculation built as to what Rockefeller's intentions might be. This wasn't your average businessman, or even your average tycoon. William Rockefeller was many things to many people at the turn of the century, and not all of them good.

He was, first of all, one of the world's richest men, just a few notches behind his brother. He was considered one of the most ruthless businessmen on the planet, as he and J.D. were the primary architects of history's most successful corporation. Their Standard Oil Trust had been formed at the expense of the lost fortunes of many others.

A number of leaders in the oil, mining, railroad, and banking industries had learned a hard lesson: little, if anything, could stand in the way of the family's money and power. The name Rockefeller had become the most hated in America. Adirondackers, and Brandonites in particular, would do well to be on the alert.

Even as the various land deals were being arranged and finalized, William Rockefeller stayed largely in the background while his purchasing agents did his bidding. Keeping a low profile in the Adirondacks would attract less negative attention, and would help keep land prices down. Rockefeller's pockets were virtually bottomless, but they didn't get that way by paying top dollar for everything.

On the other hand, no expense was too great when it came to the development of Rockefeller's compound at Bay Pond. Work was progressing at a frenetic pace, with several buildings going up simultaneously. The main cabin, when finished, would hold more than 6,000 square feet of living space, including three suites, each with its own bathroom, dressing room, and bedroom.

There was also a spacious guides' cabin finished in red birch, featuring a 540-square-foot dining room. Scattered about the immediate grounds were many other outbuildings, including a 7,000-square-foot stable and a large carpenter shop.

In the coming months, William Rockefeller imported twenty foreign deer from his estate near Greenwich, Connecticut, adding his own personal touch to the abundant natural wildlife surrounding Bay Pond. During the past seventeen years his Connecticut herd had grown to more than fifty animals, allowing him plenty of stock to transfer to the Adirondack site.

While construction progressed, William Rockefeller was at work on several other fronts, and, as some Brandon residents already suspected, there were troubled times ahead. What they didn't know was that Rockefeller indeed had a plan for the area, but their community was not part of it. When his park was finished, if Rockefeller had his way, Brandon village would no longer exist.

Considerable progress had already been made in that direction. Where a decade ago there lived more than one thousand residents of a thriving village, there were now only a few hundred people left.

Many had departed at the closure of Patrick Ducey's mill operations. Some had sold out to Rockefeller after he purchased the mill buildings and made it clear that the facility would not reopen. Others, believing they held property that was now coveted by a very wealthy man, held out for greater profit. And some stayed because it was home.

People were correct in their assumption that Rockefeller wanted their property. He was, after all, building a vast park worthy of the world's wealthiest family. But for William Rockefeller, a man accustomed to getting what he wanted, it wasn't happening quickly enough.

Holding out and trying to wrangle more money from Rockefeller was a mistake. He didn't rise to preeminence in the world of business by being easily out-maneuvered. He was a man of action, and a shrewd operator, as villagers would soon discover.

Unbeknownst to the people of Brandon, Rockefeller had already been long at work on a plan that, if successful, would force most of them to leave. While they believed their lots increased in value with each Rockefeller land purchase, he had been toiling behind the scenes in a scheme to render their properties virtually worthless.

Back in 1897, when Rockefeller selected the expanse of Adirondack land he wished to own, he made preparations for developing the area to his specifications. With plans for an estate at Bay Pond came the strong desire for privacy and plenty of elbow room. The site needed a buffer of protection wide enough that no one would be able to penetrate it.

A major feature of the region was the New York & Ottawa Railroad line that ran north from Tupper Lake to Malone. In the great woods north of Tupper Lake, the line veered east of Kildare, passing through the land now owned by William Rockefeller. After continuing north for several miles, the rail line angled northwest towards St. Regis Falls.

In that stretch of wilderness northeast of Tupper Lake stood railroad stations that were now on Rockefeller's private preserve, including stops at Bay Pond and Brandon. Many of the other smaller stations were there for the convenience of the lumber companies, like stops at Black Rapids Junction south of Bay Pond, and Madawaska and Spring Cove north of Brandon.

Since William Rockefeller desired a secluded estate, he devised a plan to move the railroad line to the west, away from Bay Pond. Such a move would serve two of Rockefeller's wishes. The Bay Pond site would become completely private and, with Brandon's mill already gone, the elimination of rail service from the south would be the *coup de grâce* for that village as well.

Brandon would be largely cut off from the rest of the world and reduced to a dead-end rail stop deep in the forest, accessible only by a spur line originating at St. Regis Falls. Property values in Brandon would automatically plummet, and Rockefeller could then buy each lot for a song, or collect them all at tax sales.

Moving an entire railroad line for one's own purposes might seem extreme to the average citizen, but not to a Rockefeller. In fact, to execute the plan, he had already set the wheels in motion nearly two years earlier.

In October 1897, at Rockefeller's request, a special commission in Malone had been appointed "to determine the advisability of discontinuing a road between the village of Brandon and Bay Pond."

The request was made under the guise of "straightening the line and eliminating a difficult grade," in spite of the fact that the very same line had operated for eleven years with few problems. The real reason for the request was to get the tracks off the Rockefeller preserve, and to eliminate rail service to

Brandon.

To urge the commission in the "right" direction, Rockefeller offered to relocate the entire section of railroad at his own expense by securing right-of-way to the west of his property and laying a new line to the north.

As an oil man, did he really wield that level of influence? Absolutely. Though most famous (or infamous) as an "oil family," the Rockefellers had deep ties in many industries. In fact, at the time, William was cultivating a growing relationship with the Vanderbilts, whose fortunes were centered in railroad ownership.

Within two years of his request to move the rail line, William became the first Rockefeller to rise from major investor to actually assume a position of power in the New York Central Railroad. He was elected as a director, and just weeks later, was voted to a position on the executive committee.

All of this had a bearing on Rockefeller's treasured Adirondack properties. In September 1897, New York State's board of railway commissioners had granted the New York & Ottawa Railroad Company permission to build a line from Moira north to the St. Lawrence River.

At the same time, a Canadian firm was building the Ottawa & New York line south to the St. Lawrence River, where the two lines were to join. It was all part of a long-range plan where the New York line would then build the final connector from Tupper Lake further south to North Creek.

From there, direct links on Delaware and Hudson lines provided rail access to Albany and New York City. The New York to Ottawa connection would become reality.

And why was all of this important to William Rockefeller? The aforementioned New York & Ottawa Railroad ran from Tupper Lake to Moira, passing right through the heart of his preserve. There would be no privacy if his park was bisected by a major rail line.

The New York Central, a Vanderbilt line in competition with the Delaware & Hudson, was adamantly opposed to the commission's decision, but their pleas had fallen on deaf ears. They had sought to maintain their domination of Adirondack rail traffic through the line operated by Dr. William Seward Webb, a member of the Vanderbilt family.

In hopes of having control of the railroad that passed through his preserve, William Rockefeller strongly supported the New York Central, but with the commission's decision made, the cause appeared lost. The New York & Ottawa had won, and the Delaware and Hudson was the beneficiary.

Then, barely two weeks after the commission's decision, the State Forest Preserve board made a stunning announcement. Through a condemnation action, they had suddenly taken control of the land the New York & Ottawa Railroad was planning to use for completing the connecting line between Tupper Lake and North Creek.

This eliminated the only remaining corridor available for the railroad. As part of the forest preserve, the land was now "forever wild." It was a shocking development.

Dumb luck? Coincidence? No. It was the typical outcome when one chose to battle against the interests of a Rockefeller. Of all the parties involved, no one commanded more influence.

With the announcement by the forest preserve board, the New York Central again controlled most of the rail traffic through the Adirondacks with lines that were already in place. And, with Rockefeller's money and his new-found power in the New York Central, his chances of reducing or eliminating traffic through his preserve were looking much brighter.

While the Malone commission continued to deliberate on the viability of the rail line between Brandon and Bay Pond, Rockefeller's hopes for abandonment of those tracks dimmed somewhat when new information came to light. Several miles southwest of Brandon, close to the borderline of Rockefeller's property, plans for a huge lumber mill had been announced.

The new mill, being built by Charles H. Turner, would be located at the settlement known as Derrick, about midway on the New York & Ottawa between Tupper Lake and Brandon.

At Derrick, Turner owned about 6,000 acres outright, and held the rights to timber on an additional 28,000 acres of woodlands in the vicinity. He had long been active in the Adirondack lumber business, and his plans for a high-capacity mill gave new life to the community of Derrick.

Turner's lumber would most likely be shipped southwest to Tupper Lake, but with the thriving community of Derrick on the line not far from Bay Pond, it would be difficult for the Malone commission to agree to Rockefeller's request that service between Bay Pond and Brandon be eliminated. Such a move would prevent access to Derrick from the north, and could prove a real detriment to its financial development.

This setback didn't deter Rockefeller in his quest to erase the village of Brandon from the map. Just as he and his brother had successfully put the squeeze on hundreds of wealthy, powerful businessmen, he would put the squeeze on the people of Brandon, and they would bend to his will.

Rockefeller's attorneys were finding it more and more difficult to convince people in the village to sell their properties. To many, Brandon was their home, and they felt an attachment to the community. To others, owning Brandon property was a ticket to making a quick buck.

It was reported initially that Rockefeller was offering market value for most properties, but there still weren't enough takers. Rather than increase the amounts offered, it was time for Rockefeller and his men to ratchet up the pressure. First, he pursued the possibility of moving the railroad line.

In spite of the uncertainty as to the Malone commission's leanings, William Rockefeller hired a team of surveyors to determine the best route north for the new section of rails that would bypass the village. The surveyors began their work in spring 1899, much to the discomfiture of locals. If Rockefeller was bluffing, he certainly was playing it to the fullest.

Attorney John Kellas, acting as purchasing agent for Rockefeller, added to those fears when he leaked information suggesting that the village could soon be faced with even more-stringent isolation. Kellas revealed he had received correspondence from many other local landowners hoping to take advantage of the Rockefeller buying spree.

If Rockefeller continued to purchase large tracts of land, Brandonites would find themselves even further from civilization. Consequently, their properties would drop precipitously in value.

In June 1899, within a few weeks of the Vilas land deal, Rockefeller's agents finally convinced the owners of two well-known Brandon hotels to sell out. One of the owners, Harrison Baker, had been a mainstay at Brandon for more than a decade, operating a hotel at the village, plus the Bay Pond House, a hunting and fishing camp on the shores of scenic Bay Pond a few miles southeast.

The move by Baker, long a community and business leader, shook the confidence of those who had hoped to remain. When he acceded to Rockefeller's pressure, other villagers soon did likewise, and Brandon's population continued its sharp decline.

(Tragically, though Baker had owned the most valued of the properties sought by Rockefeller, he had little chance to enjoy his windfall. Nearly a year to the day after the sale was finalized, Baker collapsed and died at a friend's house in Dickinson Center.)

Though the departure of Baker from the Brandon area was further demoralizing, some folks still decided to stick it out a little longer. Despite their hopes, more hardship awaited them.

Other aggressive tactics were applied by Rockefeller's men, producing a variety of results. With the purchase of each lot in the village, houses and outbuildings were sometimes torn down. If any structures were left standing, they were boarded up, and the property was prominently posted as part of the private preserve of William Rockefeller. Absolutely no trespassing was allowed.

Soon, posted signs greeted residents on the streets, on the roadsides, and on the forest fringe. It was a not-so-subtle message to everyone that it would be best to leave.

Even less subtle was the occasional disposition of entire sections of the village. When all properties in a certain area had been purchased, Rockefeller's men were sent in to burn the abandoned buildings and the piles of rubble left from those that had already been torn down. As intended, this had a powerful negative psychological effect.

Remaining residents pleaded to be allowed to use the scrap lumber for their own purposes of additions, repairs, or even as firewood. The destruction and waste were an affront to those people in need. But, the order had been given to burn it all, and so it burned.

This treatment of locals prompted some citizens to sell while they could still get a decent price. For a few, though, it stiffened their resolve to remain. If William Rockefeller was trying to make enemies, he was doing a fine job of it.

As more and more families departed, the property values of those remaining continued to drop, spurring still others to flee. With the great reduction in population came a decision in 1899 by the New York & Ottawa Railroad to remove Brandon from its regular list of stops.

The once bustling depot was now classified as a flag-stop station. Trains would pass by the village, only stopping when directed to do so by a special signal.

It was just another nail in Brandon's coffin.

In July, to the surprise of many, the usually reticent Rockefeller agreed to a short newspaper interview. He did not address the issue of Brandon's future, or lack thereof. Indirectly, he did refer to the rumors that he had purchased the Meacham Lake property, and that he had made an offer for the spectacular holdings of Paul Smith.

To clear up all the speculation, Rockefeller stated that he had no plans to increase the size of his private preserve beyond its present scope. He added that the Debar Mountain tract was purchased only as a business interest, since it still held highly valued pulp material.

Though already wealthy beyond the wildest dreams of most men, Rockefeller never stopped being a businessman. He had no need for the profit to be realized from the pulp on the Debar tract, but by spring 1900 he had a small army of 300 men cutting wood across thousands of acres.

Hauling the timber to the rail line at Loon Lake was accomplished by the newly refurbished engine that had been christened the *William G. Rockefeller* after William's third child, William Goodsell Rockefeller. William G. had joined his father in many business endeavors, and would soon be spending much time helping to develop the Bay Pond preserve.

At the age of thirty, William G. Rockefeller was a very capable young man, having graduated from Yale University in 1892. As assistant treasurer of the Standard Oil Corporation, he was no stranger to money and power, handling hundreds of millions of dollars in the name of the corporation.

NEW YORK & OTTAWA RAILROAD.

IN EFFECT JUNE 28, 1900.

14-16 Mixd. A. M.	18 Exp. P. M.	Stations.	13 Exp. A. M.	15 Mixd. P. M.
6:10	1:30	Lv. Tupper Lake Ar.	12:00	8:30
6:20	1:36	Central Jc.	11:54	8:23
†6:30	†1:46	Childwold	†11:45	†8:11
†6:40	†1:56	Kildare	†11:35	†7:58
6:52	2:14	Derrick	11:25	7:40
		Rapids Junction		
†7:08	†2:32	Bay Pond	†11:11	†7:23
7:20	2:44	Brandon	11:52	7:10
†7:34	†2:56	Madawaska	†10:507	†6:55
†7:54	†3:16	Spring Cove	†10:24	†6:32
8:08	3:28	Lv. Santa Clara Ar.	10:22	6:17
8:30	3:49	St. Regis Falls	10:05	5:54
8:40	4:01	Dickinson Ctr.	9:54	5:42
9:10	4:30	Ar. Moira Lv.	9:25	5:16
7:00		Lv. Moira Ar.	8:50	
7:22		Ironton	†8:23	
7:35		Helena	8:10	
7:45		Ar. Hogansburg Lv.	8:00	
12:00	5:08	Lv. Moira Ar.	9:33	4:34
12:28	5:30	Ar. Malone Lv.	9:06	4:07
9:33	4:34	Lv. Moira Ar.	6:56	5:08
10:15	5:30	Norwood	6:15	4:30
11:00	6:10	Ar. Ogdensburg Lv.	5:25	3:30
A. M.	P. M.		A. M.	P. M.

† Stop on signal.
Trains run daily, except Sunday.
H. W. GAYS, Gen'l Manager.
Ottawa, Ont.

The last railroad schedule with Brandon as a regular stop. The declining village population relegated Brandon to flag-stop status, joining Madawaska, Spring Cove, and others.

Of all the Rockefeller children, he was expected to be one of the major heirs to the family fortune.

In early 1900, as loggers worked the Debar tract, a somewhat amusing side note arose when a bulletin issued by the U.S. Department of Agriculture, Division of Forestry, stated that William Rockefeller was listed among the applicants for public assistance.

Clarification revealed that he had taken advantage of a federal program that prepared working forestry plans for landowners. It was part of a government initiative to eliminate the destructive logging practices that had decimated the forests of New England.

The request by Rockefeller applied to a section of the Bay Pond preserve that had not been previously logged. It contained a sizeable section of what was referred to as virgin timber, and a plan was sought using conservative methods of harvesting the stand.

So, it was true that one of the world's richest men had, in fact, applied successfully for public assistance, though he could have simply hired his own professional forester as Vanderbilt had done at Biltmore.

Both of the Rockefeller properties were very busy in early 1900. The Debar tract had yielded 12,000 cords of pulp wood, destined for the Cadyville mill owned by International Pulp and Paper Company.

Headed for the lumber mill at Onchiota was an additional three million feet of timber from Debar. After processing, it was shipped to Baker Brothers' mill in Plattsburgh.

At Bay Pond, just a year after the buildings were put into use, a surveyor was at work planning the foundation for a huge addition to the living quarters there. Eventually the complex would include several large structures, all connected by various passageways.

To complete the work, Rockefeller brought in a crew of eight workmen from his estate in Greenwich, Connecticut. In addition to constructing the large buildings, they were instructed to prepare his new game preserve.

When that was finished, Rockefeller planned to bring in

many more deer from his Greenwich location.

In recent years, William Rockefeller had been experiencing health problems, not the least of which were recurring bouts of appendicitis. Rather than continue dealing with the intense pain from each attack, and the possibility of death, he decided to have his appendix surgically removed.

During this time, he directed his son, William G., in carrying out the plans for developing his Adirondack properties.

After the surgery in late May, and a period of recovery with doctors tending to him, plans were made by William to spend the entire month of July convalescing at Bay Pond. William G. was there to handle the day-to-day needs, but his father didn't just sit idle.

Exactly a year after he publicly stated he had no plans to purchase any more Adirondack property, it was announced that William Rockefeller and his attorney, John Kellas, had partnered in a deal to purchase the 22,000-acre Everton tract located north of Brandon. The Everton site had recently been abandoned by other lumber companies, and the rail line there had been torn up and sold.

Rockefeller began preparations to harvest a large amount of hardwood at Everton, along with about 30,000 trees for sale to the pulp industry. Pulp operations were known for leaving almost nothing standing in the forest, but the current high price on the market made the deal irresistible to Rockefeller. Plans were made to get a team of men on the job as quickly as possible.

During his recovery period, William also played host to a field assistant from the forestry division, responding to his earlier request for government assistance. Work commenced removing some of the largest trees from his estate without causing undue damage to the surrounding landscape.

As both projects progressed towards year's end, news came from Brandon about the closing of another hotel. The establishment had been operated by Frank Burgess for the past three years, since about the time Rockefeller had arrived on the scene.

Burgess had served many visitors to the new private

preserve, but the population of the village had been reduced so drastically that he finally sold out to Rockefeller. With another business shuttered, Brandon moved one step closer to oblivion.

In 1901, the additions and improvements at Bay Pond continued, and by summer there stood a grand estate worthy of the name Rockefeller.

The main complex at Bay Pond was protected by a modern firefighting system. Water was piped in from streams and fed to hydrants at several locations, and hoses were placed in each building. A special bell was set up to summon all employees in case of fire, and more than one thousand feet of standard fire hose was kept at the ready for emergencies.

The Rockefeller living quarters were spectacular, and lavishly furnished. Among the elaborate structures on the grounds were a 5,000-square-foot dining building; two large guest houses; an icehouse with three cooling compartments and a capacity for 150 tons of ice; a lamp-and-oil house; and a boathouse large enough to accommodate twenty water craft. Notably, the exterior of each building was sheathed in shingles, a Rockefeller preference.

There was much more. For passage on foot or horseback, trails had been established to the far reaches of the preserve. Thirty miles of new roads also added to the ease of travel. Obstructions were removed from waterways to make them navigable, and camps were built at various locations across the preserve.

The camps were spacious, one-story structures with modern conveniences. Located on five different ponds – Follensby Junior, Long, McDonald, Quebec, and Wolf – each had several bedrooms and bathrooms, and a fireplace in every room.

It was estimated that Rockefeller had spent nearly $750,000 on improvements at Bay Pond (the approximate equivalent of $18 million in 2005). The grandeur of Rockefeller's new surroundings came as a shock to local folks, especially those of Brandon.

They were struggling to survive, and those who had long counted on the forest for food and shelter had been cut off from their basic needs. In the meantime, their new neighbor lived like a king.

Traditionally, farmers and mountain folks in the north took care of friend and stranger alike, helping each other in times of need. But in a situation like that at Brandon, things were now different.

By virtue of money, one man's desires stood above the wants and needs of an entire village. If Mr. Rockefeller had to have "neighbors," he would do his best to see that they were kept at a distance.

By this time, the Brandon story had become well known across the region. Becoming a ghost town by the natural progression of events was one thing, but being driven out to serve the whimsical wishes of a millionaire was quite another.

The Rockefeller saga had garnered plenty of media coverage, with attention focused on the private park concept. The recent proliferation of such preserves had produced a constant irritation among the general population.

In time, that irritation grew into a groundswell of opposition. After all, a man didn't need thousands of acres of land for his own use, and it was the exclusion of others from such grand tracts that was so distressing.

It wasn't just Rockefeller and Brandon, of course. The encroachment of so many powerful groups and individuals on the once-free land of the Adirondacks had been debated for many years. Passionate arguments erupted from mountain logging camps to the halls of state government. The sides were deeply divided.

Frequently, locals simply rebelled. Trespassing on private preserves became the most common of crimes, and because of his treatment of residents who wouldn't sell to him, Rockefeller's property offered a tempting target.

Some felt that by trespassing, they were fighting back, but Rockefeller upped the ante with new, oppressive tactics. Posted signs lined his property, and hired guards now patrolled his land.

And not only were hunting and fishing forbidden. No one was allowed to enter the woods to pick berries or other wild foods, or to gather scrap wood for fuel. Armed guards were instructed to confront anyone setting foot on Rockefeller property.

Since Rockefeller now owned all of the land surrounding the village, no roadways were open for use. Signs warned that all trespassers would be prosecuted.

The one highway that ran through Brandon wasn't yet posted, but its use was in question now that Rockefeller owned both sides of the road. The only sure way to legally enter or leave Brandon was by rail.

And, if Rockefeller's appeal to the Malone railroad commission proved successful, even that route would be eliminated. Surveyors were actually preparing the new rail path at that time, though the commission still remained silent.

In July 1901, Rockefeller showed that he was serious about transgressors when a popular town resident named Joe Peryea was arrested for trespassing on preserve property.

Known as "Black Joe" (of two men named Joe on a logging crew, he was the Joe with the dark hair and dark features), the man himself was not the actual culprit. Rockefeller filed suit because Joe left his horses out in the road to feed, and they had wandered onto preserve property even after continued warnings to Peryea.

Joe's best argument in court was that Rockefeller should have fenced his property if he didn't want the horses to wander onto his land. The court did not agree. After a trial, the jury found for the plaintiff and awarded six cents in damages. Peryea was also required to pay court costs.

But what stood out to the public was the pettiness of a man who owned more than 50,000 acres, yet wouldn't even share blades of grass with a few hungry horses.

Throughout the year, Rockefeller and his men continued to pressure Brandon residents to sell their property. Bitterness grew as homes were sold, buildings were torn down and burned, and posted signs lined the vacant streets.

Despite the warnings, children entered the woods to pick berries and were driven out by Rockefeller's guards. The blackberries and raspberries in the clearings, along with the late summer crop of blueberries on the pine barrens, were northern staples. Now all were left to nature. The resentment was fairly palpable.

As fall and winter approached, Brandon's people knew they were facing hard times. Decisions had to be made, and where there were young children to consider, families were forced to swallow their pride and surrender their homes.

Hatred induced some owners to refuse Rockefeller's purchase offers, preferring instead to sell their land at public auction. Others, struggling to make ends meet, eventually saw their land disposed of at tax sales rather than accept what some described as "dirty money."

As many as eight Brandon village properties were sold at one time in this manner through the Office of the State Comptroller. People felt compelled to take a stand based on principle, though they faced a painful reality. Their land still ended up in the hands of William Rockefeller.

A similar fate was averted by the Protestant Church in Brandon. Wishing to see the building preserved, parishioners dismantled it and brought the entire structure to Tupper Lake.

There it was rebuilt and reopened as the village's first Presbyterian Church. The land where it had stood in Brandon was sold, becoming part of the Rockefeller preserve.

Though most of the homes were razed and burned, many of the larger buildings that were adjudged by Rockefeller to be of some value were left standing until a buyer could be found. A typical example occurred in early 1902, when an entire structure was disassembled and hauled by train to Massena International Park, requiring nearly twenty rail cars in all. The parts were used to construct a hotel capable of housing one hundred guests.

Brandon still existed, but just barely. In a little more than two years, William Rockefeller's presence had reduced the village population to only a few families and some longtime individual residents, all of whom stubbornly refused to move. It was doubtful they could resist much longer.

4

Block 7, Lot 1

In 1898, William Rockefeller fairly burst into the North Country headlines with spectacular deals for enormous tracts of Adirondack land. Four years prior to his arrival, another important land transaction occurred in the same area. It involved only a tiny piece of property, but it would become a huge issue in the life of William Rockefeller.

Patrick Ducey was closing out his decade-long logging operations in the St. Regis Falls area in the early 1890s, disposing of his considerable holdings. As noted, he had discouraged Brandon residents from purchasing any village property, since the fortunes of the settlement were tied directly to his local business endeavors.

He believed that Brandon, like Everton before it, would become a ghost town, a casualty of the business world once his logging operations ended. After all, most of the valuable timber was gone, and Brandon village had only come into existence because of the lumber industry.

Most residents heeded Ducey's advice, but some would not be dissuaded, and Ducey agreed to sell them some land. The lots were each about one-fifth acre in size, or about one hundred feet square. Prices ranged from $25 to $100, based on the usual criteria of location and layout.

Among the buyers was a fifty-year-old lumberman and woodsman. On August 21, 1894, Block 7, Lot 1 in Brandon village became the property of one Oliver Lamora.

Our story picks up in early 1902, with Brandon village rapidly fading into oblivion. Many businesses had ceased operating, resulting in a loss of basic services. Families in particular were forced to relocate. Some residents moved elsewhere to seek employment, and others left because of the futility of their position, facing a questionable future in the remote north woods. They were surrounded by private property, and had no access to the abundant fish and game of the region.

Widespread bitterness had developed over the years about the shrinking of lands available to the public, both at Brandon and across the Adirondacks. In spite of the protests from many interests, in the end the wealthy companies and individuals always seemed to end up getting what they wanted.

Hardy individuals had slowly opened the Adirondacks, but now they were being squeezed out of the picture. Such was the situation at Brandon village.

Some chose to resist, but the victories of the common man over wealthy interests were, and are, proportionately insignificant. Yet, the adage "You can't fight city hall" has an absolutely un-American ring to it.

Truth be told, you can battle the red tape, the money, and the power, and there is always hope. You *can* fight city hall, but the reality is, you won't very often win. Most people in Brandon didn't dare try.

But Oliver Lamora was different. He loved the woods, and he loved his adopted home of Brandon. He was getting on in years, and a small pension from his service in the Civil War, supplemented by hunting and fishing, would see him through until his death.

Lamora was from tough stock, a northern woodsman of French-Canadian descent. He was born Olivier Lamoureux in May 1844, the son of Jean-Baptiste Lamoureux and Catherine Bricault (sometimes given as Catherine Lamarche). In northern New York, the name Olivier became Oliver, and Lamoureux became Lamora.

As was common at the time, the spelling of the name was Anglicized, but the original pronunciation remained relatively intact. Throughout his life, Oliver's French-Canadian heritage was evident from his thick French accent.

Part of Oliver's youth was spent in Redford, New York, a small settlement in southwestern Clinton County. Redford was a typical rural northern village, where farming and lumbering were the main occupations. As always, wild game and fish supplied part of the family's regular table fare.

On January 18, 1863, at the age of eighteen, Lamora married Ursuline-Rosalie Gagné, otherwise known as Rose. Like Oliver and thousands of other northern residents living near the U.S.-Canada international border, Rose's family was of French-Canadian extract.

On January 15, 1864, three days shy of their first wedding anniversary, Rose gave birth to a son, Oliver Jr. Both parents were still in their teens, embarking on a new life, but it was also a terrible time in American history. The nation was embroiled in a terrible Civil War, and Oliver soon made a decision that would have a lasting effect on his life.

On September 3, 1864, though he was a young man of twenty years old, all semblance of youth was left behind forever when Oliver enlisted in the Union Army.

At the time, there was an outfit based in Plattsburgh, the county seat, but Lamora enlisted at Redford, joining Company C of the 91st Regiment, New York Infantry, a unit organized at Albany, New York in 1861.

The 91st was alternately known as the Albany Regiment and the Columbia County Regiment. Oliver was among the many new recruits needed to replenish the ranks of the 91st, which had been badly decimated by illness.

In early 1865, after six months at Baltimore, the regiment was assigned to the 5th Corps, Army of the Potomac, and almost immediately saw duty on the battlefield.

After performing a supporting role in Virginia at Petersburg and Fort Steadman, the men of the 91st slogged through heavy rain and mud to face the enemy in some very intense action.

On March 31, the regiment fought in the Battle of White

Oak Road. In the morning, in the face of a furious rebel assault, the 91st was driven back and suffered many casualties. Once the troops had regrouped, another vicious battle was fought in the afternoon. Despite additional heavy casualties, the territory at White Oak Road was regained.

After a very anxious night, the 91st collaborated in a surprise attack on a large Confederate force at nearby Five Forks. Though many men were lost, the assault was ultimately successful, resulting in the capture of a few thousand rebel soldiers.

In the two days of fighting, more than 6,000 soldiers died at White Oak Road and Five Forks. The 91st Regiment lost more than 50 men, while an additional 200 were injured.

The Battle of Five Forks was a critical Union Army victory, as it exposed General Robert E. Lee's principal supply route, the South Side Railroad. Lee had no choice but to order the evacuation of Richmond and Petersburg.

Eight days later, infantry support by the 91st as part of the 5th

Battle of Five Forks lithograph depicting the clash that was pivotal in bringing about Lee's surrender eight days later (Kurz & Allison, circa 1886)

Corps at the Battle of Appomattox Courthouse proved pivotal in forcing Lee's Army of Northern Virginia to capitulate, effectively ending the war. Oliver was among the many thousands of troops to witness that historic moment when General Lee surrendered to General Grant.

Shortly after, the men of the 91st were assigned guard duty along the South Side Railroad. It was a welcome respite from events of the past several weeks, when the 91st had taken part in battles where 15,000 soldiers lost their lives.

On May 23 the regiment participated in the famed Grand Review of the Armies in Washington, D.C., a two-day display featuring military processions and all sorts of celebrations in honor of the war's end.

President Andrew Johnson, along with a number of dignitaries from the military and political realms, watched from the reviewing stand as a line of troops more than ten miles long paraded past, with young Oliver Lamora among their number.

Eleven days later, he received his official discharge, and by early July, all the men of the 91st Regiment were released to return to civilian life. Just over nine months after he had

More than 2,000 Confederate troops are marched off to prison after the Union victory in the Battle of Five Forks. The infantry, of which Oliver Lamora was a member, played a critical role in the win. (1865)

The infantry marches down Pennsylvania Avenue in Washington, D.C., in the Grand Review of the Armies, shortly after the end of the Civil War (1865)

volunteered, Oliver's military service ended. He had been to hell and back, and now it was time to go home.

Lamora returned to Redford, and he and Rose picked up right where they had left off. Almost exactly nine months after Oliver's return from the war, Rose gave birth to a second son, Xavier. Over the next two decades, the family grew to nine children, not at all untypical for the times and the region.

Eight of the children, including Louis, Rosalie (Rose), William, Edouard, George Alfred (Fred), and Mary Lena (Lillian) were born while the family lived in Redford. Samuel was born in Brandon.

While Rose handled the duties of life at home, Oliver earned a living in the woods from logging, hunting, and fishing. He built a reputation as a hard-working, efficient woodsman, toiling in the lumber camps of various jobbers.

Oliver's work forced him to follow the edge of the thinning Adirondack forest, taking him further and further from home. In the late 1880s, he was working more than thirty miles southwest of Redford, hiring out to famed hotelier Paul Smith in the St. Regis Lakes area.

Vast stands of timber there promised a long future in logging, and Smith's substantial holdings guaranteed steady employment. Eventually, to be closer to work and avoid the travel, Lamora moved the family to Brandon.

Oliver partnered with Lou Russett, also of Brandon, in running a logging camp for Smith. They proved their worth, harvesting about 1.5 million feet of timber in one season.

If there was ever a lull under Smith, there were still plenty of opportunities for employment. Patrick Ducey and other lumbering outfits generally had work available during Brandon's boom years.

By the mid-1890s, the great forest north of Paul Smith's was seriously depleted. The leaders of industry there in the past fifteen years, Ducey and Hurd, were leaving the area, and Brandon's future was in doubt. As documented, hundreds of residents had already left for greener pastures.

But for a northern woodsman like Oliver, Brandon was paradise. In beautiful, peaceful, natural surroundings, all the necessities of life were at his doorstep, sometimes literally. Sustenance came from the fish in the streams, and the plants and game of the forest. It had long been the way of the north, and that tradition suited Oliver just fine.

In all likelihood, Lamora would have lived out the remainder of his life in anonymity. But, the intense controversy that had swirled for decades over logging practices, private preserves, and public rights suddenly came home to Brandon in the person of William Rockefeller. Brandon was Oliver Lamora's home, and he had no intentions of going anywhere.

As Rockefeller slowly squeezed, drove, and manipulated people from the area, there were some who remained steadfast. They clung to their land, gritted their teeth, and struggled to survive. Oliver, however, didn't plan on struggling. As he had always done, he would seek life's necessities from the surrounding woods.

In spring 1902, the weather warmed prematurely, and ice-out (the melting of ice on Adirondack lakes and ponds) arrived early in some locations. Many of the smaller rivers and brooks were also ice-free by April 15, the official first day of trout season. More than a hundred years later, Opening Day is still one of the most anticipated events on the New York sportsman's calendar.

As he did every year, Oliver hit the trout streams of Brandon at the first opportunity. The food value of the fish may have been a necessity, but for fifty-eight year old Lamora, this was also one of life's great pleasures. What a fantastic way to spend one's closing years, fishing for trout in the Adirondack wilds.

However, as Lamora well knew, this outing on Opening Day in 1902 was no ordinary fishing trip. He had disregarded several No Trespassing signs to reach the shores of the St. Regis River. Oliver was on Rockefeller property. Fred Knapp, a guard hired to protect the private park, warned him to leave, but Oliver refused to do so until he was through fishing.

Less than a week later, on Friday, March 21, Lamora stood before a justice of the peace in Moira. Among those present were three attorneys: John Kellas for Rockefeller, and Willard and Leslie Saunders for Lamora. Witnesses included Joe Alfred of Tupper Lake, Phelps Smith of Paul Smith's, John Redwood and Eugene Flanders of Bay Pond, and Fred McNeil of Santa Clara. All would eventually play a role in the Rockefeller-Lamora battle to come.

Because of his fishing expedition, Oliver faced charges of trespassing. Hundreds of posted signs lined Rockefeller's property, attesting to the fact that no one was allowed to enter. Obviously, the millionaire meant business.

Oliver countered by claiming the river he fished in had been stocked with trout by New York State. Since the trout were public property, he had the right to access the river to catch the trout, and he had traveled the trail historically used for that purpose. Therefore, no crime had been committed.

Sensing impending defeat, Rockefeller's attorney, Kellas, asked for an adjournment, which the court granted. The intent was to recall the case when Patrick Ducey of Michigan was available as a witness. In the meantime, Oliver was dismissed.

Just six days after his first angling expedition, Lamora was once again caught fishing on Rockefeller property. For the second time in a week, he was cited for trespassing. The arguments used at Moira again stood up in court, this time in Saranac Lake. At the end of the trial, the justice ruled in favor of Oliver, and he was set free.

Kellas served notice that he would appeal the decision. Then, on May 15, Lamora was confronted by Rockefeller's guards for a third time and cited for the same infraction.

By this time, William Rockefeller was fed up with the local courts. He began making plans to pursue the case at the next level. Realizing the stakes were high, he put his attorney to work on devising a strategy he hoped would address the issue of private parks once and for all.

And Oliver continued fishing.

In the meantime, it was business as usual for William Rockefeller. On the national level, the Standard Oil Trust was the target of growing criticism, and both he and older brother John D. were beleaguered by reporters. In spite of the unwanted attention, they remained dedicated to the Trust, and continued seeking positions of power in other industries.

When summer arrived, all the families of great and not-so-great wealth returned once again to their usual haunts, with the Adirondacks among the preferred destinations. The names Roosevelt, Carnegie, Morgan, and Vanderbilt were regularly splashed about in the region's newspapers. J.D. Rockefeller passed most of the summer at Paul Smith's, while William, son William G., and other members of the family spent extended periods at Bay Pond.

Even while at play, William was always tending to business. In addition to the Lamora case, a new issue had sprung up along the southern border of his preserve. As he saw it, with his new power as a board member of the New York Central Railroad, he might be able to use the situation to control rail traffic to Bay Pond and Brandon.

Along the line of the New York & Ottawa Railroad southeast of Bay Pond, the small community of Derrick was facing a crisis. There, lumberman Charles Turner had built a huge mill as planned, bringing much employment to the area. In fact, it was Turner's mill that had brought more business to the railroad, which unintentionally decreased Rockefeller's chances of rerouting the rail line away from his preserve.

Turner had since met with some difficulty, and Rockefeller sensed an opportunity. For years, Turner had an ongoing contract with the New York & Ottawa Railroad for hauling his lumber to Tupper Lake. The railroad had recently fallen on hard times and was put into receivership. The new management, in spite of the previous agreement, raised the freight rates considerably.

Balking at the cost increase, Turner began hauling his logs southeasterly through the forest to Floodwood, about four miles distant. At Floodwood, the logs were then loaded onto the rail cars of the New York Central.

In order to reach Floodwood, the logs had to be drawn by teams of horses, but this much slower method of delivery reduced Turner's business by about half. He needed an alternative, and that's where William Rockefeller came in.

With Rockefeller's influence, a spur rail line could be built northwest from Floodwood Station to Derrick, taking all of Turner's business to the New York Central.

More importantly to Rockefeller, it would also dramatically decrease the business received by the New York & Ottawa at Derrick, perhaps boosting his chances of rerouting that line away from his preserve.

The fact that Derrick would then be accessible from the south via the New York Central might hold great sway with the Malone commission, a group that seemed to revive upon each Rockefeller request.

At the same time, Rockefeller had other business in the Adirondacks, once again grabbing the headlines. In late August, rumors abounded that he was about to purchase Meacham

Lake and the Meacham Lake Hotel in a deal that included an additional 6,000 acres of land.

Since Rockefeller might soon own the land on two sides of Paul Smith's property on the St. Regis Lakes, speculation ran wild that the Smith property itself would be his next target. If that were to happen, the Bay Pond preserve would encompass 120,000 acres of the finest territory in the Adirondacks.

The story played out across Clinton and Franklin County newspapers for several weeks. At one point, it was reported that Rockefeller had indeed purchased the entire tract, but the story proved to be erroneous.

Understandably, the misinformation appeared following the revelation that John Kellas, Rockefeller's purchasing agent, was negotiating for the Meacham Lake tract. When details of the sale were released, it was learned that the property now belonged to Kellas and two investors from New Jersey.

Though Rockefeller's financial connections aided the completion of the deal, he was not one of the new owners. He did, however, purchase the timber rights to the land. Within a very short time, Rockefeller's men were preparing a harvesting plan for the Meacham tract.

By this time, it was evident that Rockefeller wasn't just interested in a private park. He had logging teams at work near Bay Pond, on the Debar tract, at Everton, and at Meacham.

The burgeoning pulp market ascribed new value to even small trees, restoring financial potential to sites that had been heavily logged during the past decades, like the Brandon area. William Rockefeller was wringing every dollar of profit he could from the forest, even though he had long taken the position publicly that the Adirondacks must be preserved.

Logging every tract of land that he could get his hands on seemed to be accomplishing the exact opposite. And, he was already one of the world's wealthiest men. There was no need at all for him to conduct any logging operations.

Ironically, at this very time in summer 1902, Rockefeller became a charter member of the Association for the Protection of the Adirondacks (AFPA). The new group's avowed goal was to "aid in the preservation of the forests, waters, game, and fish of the Adirondacks, and to maintain healthful conditions there."

A century later, AFPA is still deeply involved in Adirondack issues. The association calls itself "the first citizen-based organization formed to protect the Adirondack region."

The implication is that the association serves as a voice for the common man, and that may be so. But the early 1900s was a different time, and the citizens that AFPA spoke for then were anything but common. This was not a grassroots organization.

Upon AFPA's incorporation in 1902, the *New York Times* said, "It is composed in membership of the owners of large private estates, parks, and preserves in the Adirondack region."

Of the thirty directors of the new alliance, to be less than a millionaire was an embarrassment. And there was hardly a preservationist among them. The names Huntington, Litchfield, Morgan, Pruyn, Vanderbilt, Webb, and Whitney were in no way confused with the real preservation movement.

Until they owned huge tracts of valuable land, most of them had little interest in saving the Adirondacks. Now, they were trying to protect what belonged to them, and because of that, some of their goals naturally were in line with those of the common man. Eventually, hundreds joined the association.

But that didn't qualify them as spokesmen for the average citizen. They fought for some popular causes, but the payoff was the right to own private parks, *exclusive* of all average citizens.

Many of them had reaped fortunes from logging their properties in the Adirondacks. Three years after its founding, former Senator Elon Brown of Watertown resigned from the association and offered a scathing review of its logging history. Among his comments were this:

> Acting on the assumption that no one but yourself has honorable intentions toward these forests ... while the great majority of the leading men in your organization are themselves engaged in denuding large tracts of Adirondack forest lands.

Rockefeller regarded himself as a conservationist since he was protecting the wildlife at Bay Pond by banning public hunting and fishing. At the same time, though, many Rockefeller family members frequently hunted and fished on the preserve.

Late that summer, Rockefeller was the target of sarcasm by a writer for the *Tupper Lake Herald*:

> An Odd Fellows' lodge in Canada has been advertising an excursion from Canadian points on the Ottawa & New York R.R. to Tupper Lake, and has issued flaming posters describing the trip as "through the beautiful and picturesque mountains at an altitude of 2,400 feet, and through Millionaire Rockefeller's extensive park, where a good view can be had of his residence and grounds from the car window, and the novelty of seeing numerous deer in the park; but no shooting allowed without special permission from Mr. Rockefeller."
>
> Whereupon the *Tupper Lake Herald* offers $5.00 and a year's subscription to any of the visitors who can obtain permission from Mr. Rockefeller to shoot his deer. Our Canadian neighbors get some peculiar ideas of things sometimes.

In autumn 1902, Rockefeller turned his attention once again to the problems at Bay Pond. With his attorney, Kellas, he made preparations to bring the annoying Lamora problem to an end, initiating action at the county court level.

In December, Oliver would face a jury on charges of trespassing, and for violating the private park law of 1896. (The 1896 law was a revised version of earlier legislation.)

There was not a huge buildup to the trial, but much was at stake. At issue was the concept of private parks in the Adirondacks, a subject that had been the center of a wild storm of controversy.

When the idea of private parks had been proposed years earlier, the preserves were clearly meant for the protection and propagation of wildlife. The best of intentions can be intricately twisted to serve a number of purposes, and somehow the "protection and propagation" was followed by other legal clauses stating that a preserve owner had the sole right to kill any of its wild inhabitants. Protection and propagation somehow became synonymous with killing, even within fenced enclosures.

In reality, it was a law for the wealthy. In the wake of the spectacular "cottages" of the rich on the shores of Newport, Rhode Island, the Adirondacks were now the place for America's affluent to have a "camp." The words cottage and camp for the wealthy had little to do with the same terms used by the common man.

Likewise, private parks had nothing at all to do with the average person, except to exclude them. Only a very rich landowner could afford to purchase, set up, and maintain a private park. It appeared that the law addressed the wishes of a very small segment of society, with no benefit to the general public. Such a law could prove favorable only to those with great resources at their disposal.

The Morgans, Whitneys, Rockefellers, et al. were past contributors to several programs intended for the preservation of New York's great forests and valuable water supply. This was an opportunity for a level of influence not available to the average citizen.

One donation alone from the Rockefeller brothers totaled $250,000, the equivalent of about $5.8 million in 2005. That kind of money was hard to ignore, nor was it intended to be ignored.

At the time, the state wanted to protect the forest preserve, but didn't have the financial resources to do it all at once. Allowing great tracts to be set aside in private parks may have seemed like an appropriate alternative, temporarily preserving the land until the state could finally afford to purchase it. Then, the civic-minded owner could sell the land to the state, adding to the public forest preserve.

That happened very infrequently. Many such tracts are still today the province of the very same families and clubs who purchased them a century ago. Often at great expense to the state (the public), some of those entities sold part of their land or granted a conditional type of access to their properties.

In the late 1800s, the men of power and wealth literally fought to defend their private parks. To keep their borders protected, they hired wardens, armed guards, and attack dogs. The line between outsider and native was defined largely by income: it was outsider (rich) versus native (poor). The debate

William Rockefeller

raged, and feelings ran deep. Neither side intended to give.

The so-called private park law was cited by Rockefeller in his efforts to prevent Oliver Lamora from fishing on his preserve. Considering the resources of Rockefeller, one of the world's most powerful men, against a Civil War pensioner, the battle at hand had all the makings of an extreme mismatch.

Representing Lamora in court was the firm of Saunders and Saunders of St. Regis Falls. Willard Jackson Saunders was the elder member, partnered with his son, Leslie M. Saunders.

Lamora's defense team was an interesting story in itself. The family surname was said to originally have been Sanders, descended from Captain John Sanders, who had been associated with the Massachusetts Bay Colony in the early 1600s.

The family also had a second unusual historical connection. During the War of 1812, a great-uncle of Willard's, Green Saunders, was reputed to have performed his own version of Paul Revere's famous ride, warning the people of the north that the British were coming.

Willard Saunders, who led Lamora's defense, had traveled a circuitous route in becoming an attorney. After attending grade school in Dickinson, he became a successful young farmer.

Later, to satisfy an interest in politics, he ran for office and was elected justice of the peace, sparking a passion for the workings of the legal system. In the late 1880s and through the 1890s, Willard practiced as a lawyer in the lower courts across Franklin County.

At around the age of fifty, he attended Moira High School to complete his education under the watchful eye of none other than Principal Leslie M. Saunders, his son and future law partner. When Willard finished high school, he and Leslie together attended Albany Law School. Leslie passed the state bar exam in June 1901, and dad did the same in October.

The firm of Saunders & Saunders was based in St. Regis Falls. Willard lived in nearby Dickinson Center and maintained a separate office in that village. Both attorneys were in great demand, sometimes working solo, but often joining forces. There were even occasions where they faced off against each other.

Oliver was aware of the Saunders' stellar reputation, and

their location at nearby St. Regis Falls ensured they were well aware of the particulars of his case, plus the attending issues.

Representing William Rockefeller was the firm of Kellas and Genaway, led by John Kellas of Malone, who had already been in Rockefeller's employ for more than four years. Kellas was one of the region's top trial lawyers and a very capable adversary.

Kellas' partner, John W. Genaway, was an up-and-coming legal star. He would go on to a very successful career as county district attorney, winning three hundred cases while losing only thirty-two over a nine-year period, before moving on to higher office. The Saunders firm clearly would have its hands full.

The two sides faced off in December 1902 before Franklin County Court Judge Samuel Beman, under whom John Kellas had studied law many years earlier. The prosecution began with Kellas presenting solid proof that Lamora had indeed trespassed on Rockefeller property on at least three separate occasions.

Willard Saunders countered with official records and witnesses certifying that the waters in question had been stocked with fish by the State of New York. It was subsequently determined that rivers containing fish stocked by the state were exempt from the park law.

An amendment allowed private parks to include waters that had not been stocked since 1895. Rockefeller had "reparked" his land under the new law, but Lamora's offenses had occurred under the old law, when no stocked streams could be "parked."

The Saunders' argument expounded further on Oliver Lamora's position taken earlier in his appearances in justice court. He claimed that public monies were used to produce the stocked fish, and once the fish were released into the St. Regis River, the public had a right to those fish. And, one couldn't be trespassing if he were gaining access to publicly owned fish.

Judge Beman agreed that every citizen had a right to pursue fish that had been stocked by the state, and he dismissed the case. It was a triumph for Oliver, and was regarded in general as a victory for the common man.

In the camps of the wealthy across the Adirondacks, the decision was viewed as a terrible wrong that had to be corrected, but that opinion collided head-on with the growing feeling among natives that the private park law should never have been passed in the first place.

Many spoke out against the law as it stood, suggesting two possible alternatives. One was to prohibit *all* hunting and fishing on private parks, even by the owners. That idea seemed to fit well with the words "park" and "preserve."

The second solution was to simply prohibit all private parks. In that way, the law would address the desires of the masses instead of the wants of the few most fortunate. The state's official policy was to preserve the Adirondacks for the benefit of all. Banning private parks within the forest preserve seemed consistent with that goal.

The usually conservative newspaper *Malone Farmer* at times expressed a surprising anti-park stance. One editorial denouncing the preserves ended with these words: "The title to all wild game is in the public, and the park law was passed supposedly in the interest of the people for the preservation and propagation of game and fish."

Early in 1903, a bill to that effect was introduced in the New York State legislature by Malone Assemblyman Halbert D. Stevens. The proposed bill by Stevens disallowed the establishment of parks encompassing any waters that had previously been stocked with state fish. It also limited the size of private parks to 5,000 acres.

As soon as the Stevens bill passed the assembly (it went no further), an opposing measure representing the interests of the millionaire camp owners was submitted. Going in the opposite direction, it sought to extend the powers of the wealthy owners.

Earlier amendments to the park law allowed preserve owners to "protect" rivers and streams that had been stocked prior to 1895. That date was later revised to 1896, and the new proposal would change it to 1897. Soon, all stocked streams would be available for inclusion in private parks.

Clearly, the rules were being tweaked to remove restrictions on land use. What would it take to satisfy these men? Collectively, they now held nearly 800,000 acres of prime Adirondack forest, removed from what had been planned as a grand public park.

The Rockefellers were among the prominent men who had

joined the movement to preserve the forests for the citizens of the state. Now, William was the owner of vast acreage, all of it closed to the public. Apparently the irony was lost on him.

In the northern Adirondacks, particularly in the Tupper Lake region, the scope of the private tracts was stunning. A public listing in March 1903 defied belief:

Name	Acres
Horseshoe Forestry Company	72,431
Hamilton Park (Whitney)	61,066
Rockefeller Preserve	52,335
Nehasane Park (Webb)	42,848
Ampersand Preserve	32,407
Everton Park (Rockefeller and Kellas)	20,000
Paul Smith's Preserve	18,484
Childwold Park	13,090
Litchfield Park	12,427
Debar Mountain Tract (Rockefeller)	11,675
Granshue Club	8,752
Kildare Club	8,536
Lake Reserves (Webb)	8,470
Meacham Lake Preserve	5,580
Grasse River Outing Club	5,520
Follensby Pond Preserve	4,855
Total:	378,476

With such enormous tracts set aside under the guise of private preserves, owners flouted the spirit of the law by using the land as their own publicly stocked game farms.

State programs supporting the propagation of deer, fish, and birds had helped wildlife to flourish, and were considered very successful. Now, whenever any of that wildlife entered a preserve, by law it became the property of the owner until it left the preserve. Some estate owners even fenced their properties, essentially taking publicly sponsored game for their own use.

Others took it a step further. The law protected the "propagation of fish, birds, and game," failing to specify that the species in question must be native, or current. Many took advantage of that loophole, digressing from a private park into more of a private zoo.

William Rockefeller brought foreign deer to his preserve, and others did the same with a variety of wild animals. The most famous of those was Edward Litchfield, who built an imposing castle just south of Tupper Lake. On the grounds of his estate was an eight-foot high fence bordering approximately eighteen square miles of land.

There, he indulged himself by collecting a menagerie of species threatened with extinction. Besides elk and moose, his critters included jackrabbits, Angora goats, quail, European fallow deer, and wild hogs. Not your typical Adirondack fare.

Such excesses made it easy for natives and politicians alike to target those apparent abuses of the law's intent. The noble idea of a great park for the people of the state had been lost somewhere along the way.

While Rockefeller sued a poor northerner whose horse strayed onto his private preserve, Litchfield brought herds of goats and packs of wild boar to the Adirondacks. It only served to reinforce the perception that some people were more equal than others. Perhaps that applied to animals, too.

In 1903 William Rockefeller was a man with many irons in the fire. Even at sixty-two years of age, he showed no signs of slowing down. While contesting a tax assessment on his New York City property (Rockefeller swore under oath that he was a resident of Franklin County, New York), and tending to Standard Oil business, he was still overseeing improvements to the property at Bay Pond, this time in the form of two lakeside Japanese cottages. An entire crew of workmen was brought from Japan to the Adirondacks to complete the work.

There was also the issue of Charles Turner's dispute with the New York & Ottawa Railroad, and his lumber shipments from Derrick to the outside world.

As board member of the New York Central Railroad, Rockefeller arranged for Turner's entire business of $20,000 annually to be handled by the station at Floodwood. A plank road was being constructed from Derrick to that location to facilitate delivery through the forest.

Tops on the agenda, though, was the Lamora court decision,

which rankled Rockefeller and his wealthy brethren. Worse, the dismissal of the suit by Judge Beman had caused a rebellion of sorts throughout the mountains.

Emboldened by Lamora's success, hundreds of trespassers had entered private parks to hunt and fish. On the Rockefeller preserve, guards recorded the names of some fifty or so violators. Similar action took place at other parks, especially in the northern Adirondacks.

But park owners fought back. Some posted the aforementioned attack dogs to protect their borders, and many hired cadres of armed guards, with orders to defend the owner's property both day and night. There were numerous threats, confrontations, and arrests. It was a terrible time for all.

Then, unbelievably, the situation worsened. What could make such a volatile, incendiary situation worse? Fire.

Fire can reduce centuries of tree growth to ashes in a short time, and this was fire on a scale never before seen in the northeast. All of the New England states, plus New York, Pennsylvania, and southern Canada were hard-hit between April and early June.

In some places, entire villages were destroyed. In Montreal, Quebec, people lit lamps in their homes in the daytime in order to see. In the shipping lanes of the St. Lawrence River, fog horns bellowed constantly as ships navigated through thick smoke.

Boaters on Lake George on the southeastern edge of the Adirondacks endured near-zero visibility. Across the region, people wrapped wet rags or towels around their faces to reduce the effects of breathing smoke and ash that fell like black rain.

New York City was smothered in a stifling cloud that spread so far offshore, fishermen came in to reach safety from what they thought was an approaching storm.

In the Adirondacks, the loss of wildlife and trees was incalculable. Drought conditions and high winds exacerbated the effects of the fire. The destruction of property was widespread, and the damage to the forest was staggering. Estimates varied as to the loss, but roughly 450,000 acres of Adirondack woodlands burned in 1903.

It was noted with cynicism that the dollar value of lost

timber would have been much higher had not vast tracts been previously denuded by logging companies.

The Brandon-Tupper Lake area was hard hit, with fire claiming about 70,000 acres, including portions of the Whitney, Brandreth, DeCamp, and Nehasane preserves. But, by far, the greatest damage was on the property of William Rockefeller.

Along Rockefeller's rail line to the Debar tract were huge piles of timber ready to be hauled away. Help was requested, and a Horicon hand engine was dispatched from Plattsburgh, about fifty miles northeast of Brandon. The Plattsburgh firemen arrived with the engine in tow, along with 500 feet of hose from Rouses Point, New York and another 1,200 feet from Albany.

The effort to save the valuable cut timber at Debar was successful, but the rest of Rockefeller's property suffered miserably. Of Bay Pond's 52,000 acres, 40,000 were damaged by fire. That number might have been lower had Rockefeller's relationship with locals been less contentious.

The acrimony that existed left Rockefeller to his own resources in defending his estate from the flames. Employees of the preserve, about fifty in number, were put to work fighting the fire, but it wasn't nearly enough. Rockefeller hired a group of one hundred laborers to help battle the blaze, and though no buildings were lost, the forest was decimated.

The battle to save the buildings at Bay Pond made headlines across the country. The debate over private parks had already been well publicized, and pretty much anything involving the Rockefellers received ample publicity. In this case, there were additional juicy details.

It was widely reported that Rockefeller's neighbors helped others in defending their properties, but none would so much as lift a finger to save anything at Bay Pond. The tactics Rockefeller had used against them, and the posting of their surroundings with No Trespassing signs, had caused strong feelings of animosity. It apparently prompted criminal behavior as well.

During the battle to save the compound at Bay Pond, it was believed that many of the fires that destroyed the woodlands were intentionally set. Arson was a very serious crime, but it certainly appeared to have played a role in the destruction of at least part of the preserve.

The majority of the larger estates, like Whitney's and Webb's, suffered fire damage on ten to twenty percent of the properties. William Rockefeller's park was scorched across eighty percent of the acreage surrounding Brandon. It was noted by those fighting the fires, including the firemen from Plattsburgh, that new blazes mysteriously kept popping up everywhere.

The saga of William Rockefeller battling forest fires played out in newspapers from Boston to San Francisco. Nearly all the coverage he received was positive, the story of an elderly gentleman, a major power broker and world-famous businessman, rolling up his sleeves and digging in to save his land.

This was news, and here's how it appeared on the front page of the *New York Times*:

William Rockefeller Now A Fire-Fighter

Travels on a Hand-Car Battling Flame in the Forests Near His Adirondack Park

Special to the New York Times

PAUL SMITH'S, N.Y. – William Rockefeller has been directing the work of the fire-fighters on his park during the last twenty-two days, and has engaged in the battles himself on frequent occasions. The buildings in the Rockefeller camp are located at Bay Pond, on the New York and Ottawa Railroad, and number about twenty. Surrounding the camp are upward of 100,000 acres of forest, which Mr. Rockefeller has been accumulating during the last few years.

Much of this land was lumbered over before he secured possession of it. He did not purchase this great tract with the object of becoming a lumberman, but worked with the men to clean the shores of the lake and the margins of the forest and to establish a beautiful summer home there, which he now claims as his legal residence. He does, in fact, pass the greater portion of his time there.

It is alleged that some of the many fires which have sprung up on the Rockefeller part in the last thirty days have been of incendiary origin, that some of the fires started from burning brush, and that others were set by railway locomotives. The dry forests are great fire traps, and the flames spread north, east, south, and west, running together at the points of ingress and egress, and making virtually a great circle of fire about the Rockefeller camp.

Railway bridges at Brandon and at Derrick, the former north of Bay Pond and the latter south of it, were burned, and trains stalled at Bay Pond while the highways were lined with burning trees.

Mr. Rockefeller directed the work of the firemen, who were divided into three gangs of about fifty men each, and himself traveled up and down the railway track on a handcar, extinguishing as many of the flames as he could, and doing all in his power to prevent their leaping across the rails and getting into other portions of the forest. There have been narrow escapes from death among the fire-fighters, who were often forced to plunge into the lakes or the streams and lie in the water while the flames passed over their heads. It is now thought that the fires are under control.

The forests are burning on nearly all sides of the Rockefeller camp, ranging from a mile to three miles from it. Some of the fires which were carried from the Rockefeller camp have approached to within three miles of the St. Regis Lakes, and there held in check by fire-fighters who are working day and night.

By the end of the first week of June, rain finally came to the Adirondacks, ending most of the major fires. The buildings at Bay Pond survived, but the Rockefeller preserve was a mess.

At Debar, the Plattsburgh firemen reported that "The fire had burned over seven miles square, and was one of the worst ever known in this section. Not a bush, tree, or living thing left; even the surface or mossy part is entirely destroyed, and nothing but the hot sand and ashes are left."

To ensure the future protection of the many structures on the estate, Rockefeller telegraphed an express order for a steam-driven fire engine. Within three hours, the new fire engine, along with 2,000 feet of hose, was on its way to Bay Pond.

As dangerous as the fires were, it was feared by some that there were greater risks facing Rockefeller, as the following newspaper excerpt reveals:

> It is now believed that the forest fires were incendiary. Paul Smith, who is a very large landowner, but is liked by the Adirondack natives, told Rockefeller he had unnecessarily made enemies and was over the danger line.
>
> "I wouldn't dare to go out," said he, "if there was such feeling against me as there is against you. I advise you to be careful of your personal safety."

Smith's warning did nothing to dissuade Rockefeller in his battle against locals. With forest fires no longer an immediate threat, he turned his attention once more to Lamora.

Four times he had taken Oliver to court, and four times he had come out a loser. As a result, his preserve had been beset by fishermen entering the property just as Lamora had done. And now it was likely that the most radical of those fishermen had aided in the widespread destruction on his estate.

In spite of the court's repeated rulings against him, Rockefeller had instructed his men to discourage all trespassers and drive them from his land. The fires may have ended, but in the Brandon area, things were just starting to heat up.

As further retaliation for the fires, posted signs were placed even on what were once main highways near Brandon, daring anyone to use them. Doubts were expressed that such a move was legal, but Rockefeller's attorneys knew it would be an effective strategy.

Their feeling was, if Brandon's residents thought it was illegal to post those roads, let them take it to court if they could afford it.

Lamora soon spoke out about the mistreatment he had

received following the court's decision in his favor. For six months since, he had been plagued by threats from Rockefeller's guards. The harassment worsened as the number of trespassers increased, which itself was attributed to Oliver's victory. Rockefeller's preserve was becoming a hornet's nest, and Lamora was seen as the blame for it all.

Finally, violence erupted when a fisherman was fired upon while on the grounds of the Rockefeller preserve. Two armed guards had thrown rocks at Samuel Barcomb, striking him while he fished. When that failed to deter him, one of the guards took aim and fired, severing Barcomb's fishing rod.

Barcomb escaped the incident without injury. The gunman, said to be a crack shot, claimed to have struck his intended target. Barcomb filed a legal complaint, and the two preserve guards were arrested on charges of second degree assault. While awaiting grand jury action, both men were released on bail.

Meanwhile, the northern Adirondacks were in an uproar. The actions of Rockefeller's guards caused widespread outrage. Newspapers reported that "At Tupper Lake, citizens there have organized a club to be known as the Adirondack Game and Fish Protective Association, and say they will fight Rockefeller and his methods and henchmen at all hazards."

It was a very volatile situation, and Rockefeller did little to defuse it. In fact, quite the contrary. He kept the pressure on from all sides, and soon received news that further invigorated his campaign. The state appellate division had reversed the lower court's ruling, returning the issue to county court for retrial. The legal battle was not over.

But that wasn't enough. Adding fuel to the fire, Rockefeller successfully sought an injunction barring Lamora from all Rockefeller property. The Saunders firm was outraged at how William Rockefeller was continuously attacking Lamora, and they began the fight to have the injunction lifted.

In the meantime, the court's ruling had a stifling effect on the old woodsman. Because Rockefeller owned all of the surrounding property, including the streets of Brandon, Lamora was virtually a prisoner in his own home.

By law, Oliver was allowed passage to the train station

in Brandon, and he could use the main highway that led south ten miles to Paul Smith's by way of Keese Mills. Setting foot anywhere else would land him in jail, and put him at risk of retaliation by Rockefeller's guards.

Though the higher court ruled in favor of Rockefeller regarding the trespassing violations, it went much further in clarifying the intent of the law. The proffered explanation was very difficult for the public to accept, and it was feared that severe repercussions would result.

Earlier, the lower court ruling basically held that the public must have free access to fish that were raised for public consumption. It was not legal for any individual to claim public game as his property, though he could own the property on which the game roamed.

The higher court turned that ruling inside out, saying the state could not take a man's land by stocking it with fish or game. If the fish or game wandered onto private property, the law could not allow public trespassing in pursuit of the publicly sponsored game. In the words of the court:

> Our interpretation of the statute is that the stocking of streams and waters ... in order to give the right to the public to fish therein, must be with the consent of the owner ... and that the public is not permitted to follow the migration of the fish and take them in that part of the stream on private lands without the owner's consent.
>
> The court recognizes the fact that the title to wild game and fish is not in the park owners, but at the same time clears away the cobwebs surrounding the exclusive right of owners to fish in their private streams. No man owns wild game or fish, even though they be on his land, unless he has reduced them to his possession by capture. If they wander from his premises to those of the public or another, he may not complain of their taking.

In essence, the court held that a public river became private when it crossed private land, and that exemplary damages were appropriate to address violations of the game law.

In the opinion of the higher court, private property rights must be maintained above all, and to do so, property could not legally be stocked without the permission of the owner. No evidence had been offered in Lamora's case to indicate there had been owner consent.

The ruling by the justices was not in keeping with the long-held concept of the Adirondacks as a public park, and surprisingly, they said as much in their decision. But, the court felt that their interpretation of the law was necessary to protect the right of private land ownership.

The court's final words offered a stinging rebuke to the natives of the Adirondacks, who for ten years had shared in the great public park experiment. Said the justices:

> We are mindful that this interpretation deprives the public at large, by the infliction of severe penalties for infraction of the law, of the pleasure and profit of fishing and hunting in a very large portion of the Adirondack forest, and gives to men of great wealth, who can buy vast tracts of land, great protection in the enjoyment of their private privileges.

It was a slap in the face for the common citizen, and a great victory for the most fortunate of society. For years the issue of allowing public parks had been debated, drawing a clear battle line not only between the rich and the poor, but between the rich and everyone else. And, in general, money wins.

But it isn't always easy.

Some hoped the court's latest ruling was just the tonic needed to end the debate and bring the trespassing violations to an end. That didn't happen. Instead, it further inflamed an already combustive situation.

Arrests continued on estates across the Adirondacks, most of them resulting in convictions. But this was another game the violators couldn't win. Their pockets were shallow, while those of the rich were bottomless.

Still, the infractions persisted for a time, and many fines were imposed. The loss of $100, or even $25, could be devastating to a family struggling to get by. But a clause in the private park law allowed for exemplary damages, half of which went to the complainant, and the other half to the state.

Exemplary damages, in modern lingo, are more often referred to as punitive damages. They are intended as punishment, and to set an example for others as to what fate awaits them for a similar infraction.

The private park law provided for a maximum fine of $25 per violation. It also allowed judges to require a convicted defendant to pay court costs, which alone could be far more substantial than any fine.

In spite of the costs to offenders, cases of game law violation and trespassing were frequent. Many poor Adirondackers watched their hard-earned cash go into the coffers of Rockefeller, Vanderbilt, Morgan and the like. It was painful punishment, and very difficult to accept.

Samuel Barcomb, who had trespassed, fished, and been fired upon on the Rockefeller preserve, found himself deeply affected by the court's ruling. Those who had fired gunshots towards him had been arrested, but now it was Barcomb who was summoned to court for having repeatedly trespassed on Rockefeller property.

Since the incident, Barcomb had fallen on hard times financially. He had little more than the clothes on his back, and twice he failed to show up for scheduled court appearances. Rockefeller's attorney, John Kellas, stood before Justice R.H. McIntyre in Saranac Lake, presenting evidence of the violations, and seeking $200 in damages.

The jury heard the case, and in the absence of a defense or a defendant, rendered their verdict. Barcomb was found guilty of multiple violations, twenty-three in all, and fined a total of $200, despite his financial status.

Rare was the common man who could pay such a fine, but not to worry. To ensure punishment of Barcomb, an order for body execution of the sentence was requested by Rockefeller's attorney and issued by the court.

Body executions were generally applied to defendants who refused to comply with a court order. They were taken into custody and held until they agreed to honor the court's ruling.

In Barcomb's case, a body execution meant something different. If a defendant was found guilty and lacked the money to pay his fine, the law provided an alternate penalty of one day in jail for every dollar of the fine that remained unpaid.

This exposed another great inequity of the justice system, often imposing far greater punishment on people of ordinary financial means. A wealthy person could simply pay a fine of $200 and walk away, having been mildly inconvenienced.

To a poor person, the very same punishment could have devastating, long-lasting effects. No matter what the issue, it seemed that money always offered advantage.

During that turbulent summer of 1903, preserve guards remained vigilant and lawyers handled frequent court cases for trespassing. Wealthy park owners, with family and friends, continued to enjoy pleasures that were once the sole province of mountain residents, who were now being pushed aside.

Oliver Lamora and his ilk could not fish or hunt on private preserves, but it wasn't because men like Rockefeller wanted to protect the wildlife. It was because of who they were, a distinction of class. Natives, poor locals, and even Rockefeller employees were not allowed to hunt or fish on Rockefeller property.

Yet, from Adirondack newspapers to the *New York Times*, reports were frequently published describing wildly successful fishing trips at Bay Pond and on other private preserves.

Here's a typical example from a multitude of choices: "Mr. and Mrs. Appleton Robbins visited Follensby Junior upon the invitation of William Rockefeller, and there caught twenty-one speckled beauties, weighing from two to two-and-a-half pounds each."

For those who were once accustomed to the pleasure, but now denied, it was akin to pouring salt in the wound.

As fall arrived, men and women alike prepared for the coming hunting season, always an exciting time.

On September 19, 1903, everything changed when a single bullet took the life of millionaire Orrando Dexter twelve miles northwest of Brandon.

5

Murder in the North

Orrando Perry Dexter was born into wealth and, like his father, became a millionaire. In the 1880s, he sought a private, quiet, country home where he could follow his favorite pursuits: the study of mathematics, and a deep interest in genealogy. He was an accomplished genealogist, credited with several publications, some of which applied to the Dexter lineage.

In many other respects, Dexter's story in the northern Adirondacks closely paralleled William Rockefeller's. Much like Rockefeller coveted Bay Pond, Dexter had set his sights on a beautiful body of water known as East Branch Pond.

His first land purchase in the area came in 1886, near Santa Clara. Then, on January 4, 1887, it was announced that Dexter had acquired an adjacent tract of 911 acres, including East Branch Pond, which he renamed Dexter Lake.

(The lake and surrounding acreage gained fame a century later when it became the property of singer Shania Twain and husband Mutt Lange in the 1990s.)

What Dexter had purchased was a very popular hunting and fishing ground. Dexter Lake formed the third point of a nearly equilateral triangle touching on St. Regis Falls about four miles directly north, and Santa Clara about four miles northeast. The lake and its environs had long been a favorite of locals from those two villages.

Dexter immediately announced plans to build a grand residence on the shores of the lake. Without delay, building materials were brought to the site, including bricks, cement, and soapstone for a huge fireplace. For the framework, Dexter ordered 32,000 feet of lumber from a nearby mill. It appeared that locals might benefit from the project in some respects.

But Dexter soon made it clear that he was not seeking the company of friends and neighbors. He wanted a private estate where no one would bother him. To that end, like Rockefeller, he posted his property and sought more land as a protective buffer. Thus began a relationship based on bitterness and resentment, resulting in many head-to-head battles with local residents.

Dexter was every bit as litigious as Rockefeller proved to be, in fact, even more so. As his holdings grew to several thousand acres, Dexter spent as much time in court as he did on his estate. He sued locals for trespassing, illegal hunting and fishing, eviction from property, breach of contract, and arson (for setting fire to his land).

Besides the many trespassing sportsmen he took to court, Dexter also sued logging companies, the deputy sheriff, the sheriff, and the district attorney. For five consecutive years, he sued the town assessor. He filed suits for malicious prosecution, false imprisonment, conspiracy, and malfeasance in office.

Orrando Dexter was not a man to back down from anyone. He fought battles through all levels of the court system, and even took his case against the district attorney all the way to the governor's office.

Any decision lost by Dexter was immediately appealed, and the appeals continued until all forums were exhausted. This was a very contentious man, familiar to a wide range of judges and lawyers. (John Badger, a favored attorney of Dexter's, seemed aptly named to handle the affairs of such a tenacious fighter. John Peasley Badger was a well known, successful Franklin County lawyer.)

Dexter was also on the receiving end of several suits, with charges including destruction of property (he physically tore apart a dam upstream from his estate, meant to divert water from his land), malicious prosecution, false imprisonment, and libel. Though he was an attorney himself, he regularly hired others to represent him in court.

Orrando Dexter was known to use some nasty tactics to get what he wanted, and again, a parallel can be seen to the Rockefeller story. One incident provides an unusual look inside the workings of a millionaire's mind.

Dexter once coveted a particular piece of property that bordered his own, which by then had grown to an estate of about 3,000 acres. The owner, Warren J. Alfred, had already begun logging operations when Dexter came forward with an offer. Alfred considered the amount to be low, so he declined to sell, and continued his logging operations.

Dexter intended to have the land, and when he couldn't convince Alfred to sell, he went on a rich man's buying spree, purchasing all of the land surrounding Alfred's. If nothing else, it proved a decade later that Rockefeller's strategy at Brandon village was not unprecedented.

Once Alfred's property was enclosed within his own, Dexter then provided the final indignity. He built a house on the new land, smack dab in the middle of the only access road to Alfred's woodlot. As a finishing touch, he manned the house with armed guards.

As soon as Alfred set foot upon Dexter's property, he was charged with trespassing. Little did the lumberman know he had stepped into a trap. It was all part of an elaborate plan to wrest his property from him if he dared take on Dexter's wealth and legal know-how.

Soon, Alfred was served notice to appear in court, not in Franklin County, but in New York City! Dexter had taken advantage of the law requiring a plaintiff to file suit at either of two locations: the site of the transgression, or his place of residence.

He chose the latter, since he knew Alfred would be financially stung and deeply inconvenienced by the travel required. For Dexter, going to New York City was just another trip home.

Alfred was forced to file suit for a change of venue, which he won, but only after Dexter filed appeals all the way to the State

Supreme Court. His delaying tactics were riling, but extremely effective.

For four years the issue was contested in various courts, and when Dexter finally won, he even appealed the terms of his own victory. The court had upheld his suit, but awarded him only six cents in damages. The latest appeal added another year to the case, and Dexter was ultimately victorious, receiving an award of $125 plus costs, which added $800 to Alfred's bill.

Of course, Alfred appealed *that* decision, adding yet another year to the litigation. After more than five years of suits and countersuits, the matter finally ended when the State Court of Appeals upheld the terms of the settlement. Alfred's land was sold at public auction. The buyer was Orrando Dexter.

The financial cost to Dexter in the Alfred suits far outweighed the monetary return, but that wasn't the point. To him, winning was imperative, no matter what the cost. The same could be said for his ongoing battle with those who trespassed on his land, since he took each transgressor to court. In the end, the constant litigation cost him his life.

By the year 1900, Dexter was already long established as the most hated man in the north, but William Rockefeller proved a worthy competitor for that title. As Rockefeller's actions against Brandon village and Oliver Lamora riled the masses to new heights, Dexter expanded his estate by 3,000 acres in late 1902, further angering locals.

His latest purchase cut off several privately owned tracts of timber positioned within Dexter's land, identical to the situation that had existed with Warren Alfred a decade earlier. Dexter regularly refused requests to haul timber across his property or to float it on any streams. Held in isolation, the properties were now virtually worthless.

The apparent disdain that rich men like Dexter and Rockefeller exhibited towards the common man finally boiled over. Dexter had received repeated threats on his life, but had taken few obvious precautions.

On the day of the shooting, September 19, 1903, three vehicles were readying for travel from the Dexter Lake property. The first, a horse and buggy, carried estate Superintendent Azro

M. Giles, along with a mason who had been working at the site.

Orrando Dexter was the sole occupant of the second horse and buggy. The third vehicle was a larger wagon driven by Bert Russell, another employee. Dexter left a few minutes behind the Giles wagon, and Russell was still preparing to leave the barn when he and some other employees heard two gunshots, but thought nothing unusual of it.

A few minutes later, Russell drove off and soon came across the body of Dexter lying on the ground, motionless. Russell called out for help at about the same time that Azro Giles reached the main road and noticed Dexter's unmanned buggy coming up behind him.

Giles at first suspected that Dexter had accidentally fallen from the buggy. But then he saw blood all over the seat, and he immediately hurried back towards the estate. By the time Giles reached Russell where the body lay, Dexter was already dead.

The sheriff, the coroner, and John Badger, Dexter's attorney, were immediately summoned, and an investigation was begun. It didn't take long to determine what had happened.

As Dexter had driven through a wooded area not far from his home, someone had stepped quietly from the trees after the buggy passed, and then fired two shots.

One bullet passed through the buggy seat, struck Dexter in the back,

Orrando Perry Dexter, William Rockefeller's millionaire neighbor to the north, and victim of an assassin's bullet

passed completely through him, and struck the horse's rump.

Even then, the bullet still retained enough velocity to bury itself twenty-two inches deep within the horse, one of Dexter's prized animals. The horse raced off, and after about a quarter mile, Dexter's body fell from the buggy.

Later, the horse had to be euthanized, and the bullet, a .38 caliber slug, was removed by a veterinary surgeon.

As word of the murder slowly spread, shock and fear gripped the region. People of the north braced themselves for what might come next.

Even Attorney Badger, the victim's friend and legal counsel, acknowledged that Dexter had made many enemies over the years with constant litigation over multiple issues. Dexter always felt that he was simply defending his property.

In spite of that observation by Badger, he didn't believe that the killer was one of those past victims of Dexter's court actions. He surmised that the shooting was likely prompted by Dexter's recent acquisition of the 3,000 acres that negatively affected the finances of several lumbermen. That expansion had generated many hostile comments, rekindling the hatred towards him.

Among Badger's candid comments was this:

> The motive for the crime was revenge for some real or fancied wrongs suffered by somebody. Mr. Dexter had many enemies because of his relentless warfare against game poachers, timber cutters, and trespassers. He had so much litigation, and many a woodsman felt bitter against him. Some of these men had made threats against Mr. Dexter's life, and naturally they are under suspicion.

No one expressed surprise that Dexter had been shot, considering his well-known abrasive history of the past ten years, but all were dismayed that the deteriorating situation had descended to the level of cold-blooded murder.

Orrando Dexter's father, ninety-year-old Henry Dexter, was founder and president of the American News Company, and himself a millionaire many times over. Shortly after the shooting, Henry came forward with a reward of $5,000 for information leading to the capture and conviction of his son's killer.

Elsewhere, reaction was immediate. The sixty wealthy members of AFPA offered unlimited financial assistance in finding and capturing the murderer. It was a substantial offer. The membership roster included dozens of millionaire landowners.

Meanwhile, lawmen continued searching for clues to the killer's identity. Had it occurred at the height of the summer season, the shooting could well have sparked a panic among the visitors who thronged to the Adirondacks each year.

As it was, the news caused a substantial stir among the late-season fishermen and early hunters and their families. Upon hearing of the murder, many left immediately.

Though small in number, there were a few camp and estate owners who allowed hunting and fishing on their preserves, usually by a permit system. It was generally believed that those individuals had no reason to be alarmed.

At other camps, a siege mentality ensued. Primary among them was the Bay Pond estate, just twelve miles southeast of where Orrando Dexter had been shot dead.

There was reason for fear. William Rockefeller's history near Brandon was very reminiscent of the Dexter story that had played out in local newspapers for more than a decade.

In fact, shortly after Dexter's murder, Franklin County authorities were quoted as saying that they had "long been anticipating such a crime as the assassination of Mr. Dexter." They further indicated they had feared William Rockefeller would be the first to fall victim to an assailant, not Mr. Dexter.

How disquieting it must have been for Rockefeller to read such comments in the media. Of course, there were other newspapers that supported the wealthy businessmen and landowners. Comments such as this one received much play:

> William Rockefeller, who has been regarded as a marked man throughout the region, has won admiration by his bravery in going to his estate in Franklin County on hearing of Mr. Dexter's murder. Villagers make no secret of the fact that his life is in imminent peril, but Mr. Rockefeller carries himself

> with utter disregard for the assassin's bullet. He has
> an estate of 50,000 acres of virgin forest, which he
> has rigorously closed against hunters, fishermen,
> game poachers and visitors.

There were many in the northern Adirondacks who resented being portrayed in the media as ruffians, savages, and killers. But there were also some who adopted a wait-and-see attitude. The killing of Dexter was wrong, but maybe it would serve as that defining event that would effect change to the private park law, and stop rich people from driving off the common man just so they could have their own playground.

In the immediate aftermath of Dexter's demise, there was no sign of such change. If anything, the opposing sides were even more entrenched. Rumors abounded of threats, fights, and shootings on private preserves, including Rockefeller's.

In spite of the claims that Rockefeller did not fear his enemies, many protective measures were taken at Bay Pond. No longer a bastion of privacy, the lakeside compound was now lit almost as brightly at night as in the daytime.

The staff of armed guards was increased, some of whom were assigned to patrol the streets of Brandon, where barely seventy-five residents remained.

Of course, there were fewer streets to patrol in the village, since by this time, Rockefeller's men had torched more than fifty homes after he had purchased them during the past four years.

Despite the claims of a defiant, fearless attitude in the face of danger, William Rockefeller was nowhere to be found, leaving Superintendent John Redwood in charge at Bay Pond. Redwood, long a Rockefeller friend and employee, hired detectives from a firm in New York City to ensure the family's safety.

Of the many guards on the estate, a dozen heavily armed men provided constant security near the residences at Bay Pond, while others patrolled the surrounding grounds.

But 50,000 acres was just too large an area to cover. Reports continued to come in of gun-toting strangers invading the preserve's boundaries, and the situation assumed an air of desperation. Ironically, the millionaires were virtually prisoners in their own home, much like Lamora was virtually imprisoned in his home by Rockefeller's injunction.

Confidants and advisors encouraged the Rockefeller family members and guests to leave, lest Dexter's fate befall them, too. The anxiety grew to unbearable intensity, and the danger was real. Nine days after Dexter's murder, the family fled the compound.

Rather than await the regularly scheduled train and assume great risk by traveling on public transportation, a special train was assigned to take the entire group from Bay Pond to New York City.

A day earlier, it had been announced that William Rockefeller was heading north for his Adirondack estate, but reporters waiting at Paul Smith Station at Brandon were disappointed to discover that neither he nor his son, William G., had made the trip from Tarrytown, the family estate along the Hudson River. It was widely reported that death threats prompted their decision to stay away.

The escape from the Adirondacks received headline coverage across the country in all the major newspapers. "Rockefellers Flee to City" and "William Rockefeller Fears Assassination" greeted readers who followed the story. For a man of William Rockefeller's stature, it was deeply embarrassing.

The exciting headlines attracted many new readers eager to consume the saga of the rich, powerful businessman versus the mountain villagers and their symbolic leader, Oliver Lamora. It was a modern-day version of David and Goliath, and the public loved it.

With his land recently ravaged by fires, many of them intentionally set, and the murder of Dexter, a like-minded, wealthy individual, Rockefeller's utopia was in deep trouble. And now he and his family had been driven from the Adirondacks, at least temporarily.

It certainly looked like a good time to lie low for a while, but besides his business interests and the problems at Bay Pond, another court case involving William was imminent. Coming soon was Round 6 of Rockefeller vs. Lamora.

When the appellate court had ruled against Lamora, it

also returned the trespass charge to Franklin County Court for retrial. Lamora had previously won that argument based on the public's right to waters stocked with fish that had been raised by the state.

The appellate court determined that ruling to be correct only if the waters had been stocked with permission of the owner. That particular issue would have to be addressed if Lamora was to have a chance of winning again.

In December 1903, one year after the initial county trial, two outstanding attorneys faced off once again, John Kellas for the prosecution and Willard Saunders for the defense.

In a trial that lasted nearly three days, Kellas called only two witnesses, largely standing on the merits and arguments of the case that had been upheld by the appellate court. Lamora had indeed trespassed after "having ignored warnings a hundred times or more," according to Kellas. Because Oliver disregarded repeated warnings, Rockefeller was within his rights to sue for trespassing.

Lamora's testimony revealed the harassment he had been subjected to by Rockefeller's men, even after the court had repeatedly ruled in Lamora's favor. He described his small house in Brandon on one-fifth acre of land. He told the court that Rockefeller's agent ordered him to "leave the town or he would soon law him out of it."

That was no idle threat, especially coming from a powerful millionaire against a poor Civil War pensioner.

Willard Saunders had done his homework, now presenting new evidence that he hoped would sway the jury to Lamora's viewpoint. Saunders called a total of seven witnesses in an effort to satisfy the arguments earlier found lacking by the higher court.

First, proof was provided that the waters had been stocked by the state, using fry from the hatchery at Saranac Inn, something Saunders had already proven in the earlier trial. This information was confirmed by Grant Winchester, manager of the hatchery facility.

Then, Saunders offered evidence that the waters had been stocked with the owner's permission: not William Rockefeller, but Patrick Ducey!

As the owner of the property previous to Rockefeller, Ducey had not only allowed the stocking to take place. He had even provided officials with the use of his own horse to bring the fish to the stocking sites.

Saunders then claimed that when Rockefeller purchased the property, he was bound by the acts of the previous owner. With state stocking and owner permission established, Saunders then launched a passionate assault on the private park law, questioning its constitutionality before resting his case.

It was a brilliant performance. After only thirty minutes of deliberation, the jury decided there was "no cause of action." Lamora had won again.

Of course, Rockefeller would appeal. After all, his case could determine the fate of private parks throughout the state. But for the moment, at least, Lamora was back on top.

Most Adirondackers did not know it at the time, but the situation involving Brandon and Oliver Lamora was not unique in William Rockefeller's experience. Three hundred miles south, a similar situation was occurring near Tarrytown, a small village of fewer than 5,000 residents just twelve miles north of the New York City line.

Long before the wealthy men of America discovered the Adirondacks, they had sought refuge in Tarrytown, escaping the stifling atmosphere of the city. The area was nicknamed "Millionaire's Colony," the site of sixty-five spectacular estates, complete with mansions and castles.

William and J.D. Rockefeller had purchased smaller adjoining estates there, gradually expanding as they bought out neighbor after neighbor. Then came the pressure tactics, much as were employed at Brandon. No matter how long it took, the Rockefellers were united in their cause and persistent in their efforts. Yet, they often refused to negotiate prices.

In one instance, J.D. offered an owner $1,800 for his property, but the man wanted an even $2,000. As much as he wanted the land, Rockefeller, the world's richest man, refused to budge on his offer. For two years he waited. When the man finally realized Rockefeller would not yield, he sold out for the

William Rockefeller's childhood home in Richford, New York

William Rockefeller's castle home at Tarrytown, New York. Of all the spectacular Tarrytown mansions, Rockefeller's was the largest with 204 rooms.

original offer of $1,800.

The Rockefeller brothers were single-minded in their goal of eliminating all neighbors they considered undesirable. One victim stood strong for nearly a decade, fighting to retain his property bordering the Rockefeller land. With William's full support, older brother John led the assault.

Throughout the lengthy ordeal, J.D. continued to make his opponent's life miserable until, beset by personal tragedy and spent from the constant harassment, the man finally surrendered.

John Melin, his spirit broken, told his story to the *Washington Post*. Following is an excerpt from the front-page news item:

ROCKEFELLER WINS

Tarrytown Saloon-keeper Finally
Gives Up His Long Fight

Special to The Washington Post.
New York, Sept. 14.—"Rockefeller always wins," sighed J.J. Melin, of North Tarrytown today. "How can you beat him? If he can't knock you out, he will tire you out. I am going away from here."

J.J. Melin has lasted for eight years in his little liquor saloon on the boundary of the Rockefeller estate. He has fought John D. Rockefeller in the courts and at the polls. He has beaten the billionaire in elections, but he has lost all appetite for fighting. He is lonesome.

"Everything comes Rockefeller's way," explained Melin. "About a year ago my wife died. I thought everything of my wife, and when she died I was sad. I could not stay around the place; it was so lonesome. Then my sister came here to live with me, and, about two months ago she died. I have nothing left to hold me around here.

"I was here before Rockefeller came. For twenty-one years I have lived right in this place. Rockefeller started to drive me out, but he could

not, because this is a free country. There is a limit
that even a rich man can't run over. But he never
gives up, that Rockefeller. One by one he bought
out all my old friends around here and they moved
away. I wouldn't sell. He kept on buying out my
old friends and clearing their land, and they moved
away.

"Now I am going to sell out, but not to
Rockefeller. I always said I wouldn't sell out to him,
and I wouldn't sell out to anybody now if it wasn't
so lonesome. But I can't stay here all alone."

Undoubtedly an agent of John D. Rockefeller
will pick up the Melin property and drive out of
the community of the Rockefeller estate the only
saloon within reaching distance of his employees.

When William Rockefeller fled the Adirondacks after
the Dexter murder, he joined J.D. for a time at their estates
in Tarrytown. It wasn't all peaceful there, either. William and
J.D. together had recently formed the Tarrytown Gun Club,
with membership limited to the area's wealthy landowners. The
Rockefellers' club was soon enveloped in controversy.

Just as was done in the Adirondacks, all private estate lands
were posted, effectively eliminating locals from their traditional
hunting grounds. To prevent poaching, the club hired guards
and outfitted them with rifles. The whole scenario certainly did
have a familiar ring to it.

During William Rockefeller's hiatus from the north,
John Kellas was preparing to return to court over the Lamora
trespassing issue. He was also handling other Adirondack
entanglements for Rockefeller, including a suit against the St.
Regis Paper Company, and another against an independent
hotel owner not far from Bay Pond.

In the hotel case, an elderly Adirondack guide by the name
of John Whitcher had opened a small summer roadhouse on the
shores of the St. Regis River, about two miles north of Brandon
on a piece of land he had purchased from Patrick Ducey. This
irked Rockefeller, for here was another difficult local who refused
to sell his property.

And not only was Whitcher running a business that would bring others close to Brandon village. He had also secured a liquor license, something that Rockefeller was dead set against, as were John Hurd and Patrick Ducey before him. He certainly didn't need liquor fueling the anger of his enemies.

On Rockefeller's behalf, the ever-efficient Kellas did some background work on the Whitcher property. Kellas discovered that one of the terms of sale inserted by Ducey prohibited Whitcher from selling alcohol from the site for twenty-five years. Kellas obtained a court injunction restraining Whitcher from trading in alcohol, severely injuring his business.

Rockefeller also did his part to keep the natives stirred up, revealing yet another tentative plan to eliminate the rail line through Brandon. This new effort was tied to the announcement that partners Paul Smith and Wallace Murray were expected to build an electric railroad east of the village of Brandon, extending from Meacham Lake all the way to Lake Placid.

Rockefeller revealed that, with the completion of that line, he would then run a branch northwest to St. Regis Falls, bypassing Brandon and his beloved Bay Pond estate. He also planned to build an overhead trolley to connect the electric railroad to the New York Central.

Most of the proposed schemes never came to fruition, but the positing of each scenario kept Brandon village in turmoil.

Actions like that against John Whitcher, plus the new plan to move the railroad, prompted some people to leave the Brandon area, but it also strengthened the resolve of those like Black Joe Peryea and Oliver Lamora.

Peryea remained a thorn in Rockefeller's side for a variety reasons. He owned several other buildings besides the Brandon House, which also included a small store, and he made it clear to Rockefeller that he would not part with any of his properties.

Peryea normally resisted within the law, but occasionally resorted to guerilla tactics. For instance, Rockefeller once built a tower in the village so that his guards had a sweeping view of the surrounding area.

From their high perch, they could watch for fires, but just as important, they could keep a close watch on the few remaining village residents, and perhaps catch them sneaking onto Rockefeller property. The tower didn't last long, and its disappearance was said to have been the work of Peryea.

The Lamora case was particularly irritating to Rockefeller. Originally, when Kellas had contacted locals about selling their property, Oliver had asked for $1,500. He owned a house that was larger than most in the village, and it sat on a lot measuring perhaps one hundred feet square.

Lamora knew of Rockefeller's great wealth and saw a chance to turn a good profit. Kellas had asked for two days to think about the offer, and Lamora told him to take three.

Those were the last civil words to pass between the two sides. When Lamora next encountered Rockefeller's men, he was threatened with legal action if he didn't sell out, details of which he later revealed in court.

The implication of the threat was clear. Legal action was a common bullying tactic used against people of limited financial means. For the average citizen, the prospect of going to court was very intimidating, and could be financially devastating.

The fact that millions of dollars stood behind Rockefeller's threat made it even more onerous. His track record in court was flawless, and he would use that capability to get rid of Oliver.

With that, Lamora dug in his heels. He wasn't going anywhere, and swore the price for his property was now $5,000. His stance bore no subtleties. He was firmly entrenched within the village. This was a battle of wills between two men of widely disparate backgrounds and means, but equal in stubbornness.

With the Whitcher case behind him, Kellas was preparing to meet Lamora in court yet again. The decision in favor of Oliver was back in the hands of the appellate division by virtue of Rockefeller's second appeal.

In the meantime, Lamora was seeking to have the restrictive injunction lifted so he would be free to leave his home. Kellas would fight to keep it intact.

W.J. Saunders was a very eloquent spokesman on Lamora's behalf, and he bristled at the way his client had been treated. No matter if the court ruled in Rockefeller's favor or against him, he continued to inflict harassment upon Oliver through his

William and John D. Rockefeller (1907)

preserve guards.

When Lamora's neighbor across the road offered his property for sale, Rockefeller purchased it. Instead of following the usual practice of tearing the house down, he set up quarters there for Eugene Flanders, a preserve guard, now in a great position to keep a close eye on Lamora's every movement.

Lamora claimed that Flanders was put there to spy on him. Like most Rockefeller tactics, it was unethical, aggressively annoying, and perfectly legal. The constant pressure of the agitation, plus the intense court battles, should have demoralized Lamora, but he stood strong in the face of it all.

Financially, though, it would have taken literally a half-million bankrolls the size of Lamora's to match Rockefeller's money. There were attorney fees to pay, and Lamora, now sixty years old and surviving on a small Civil War pension, was a poor man. The cost of litigation had already drained his savings, and his meager income left him little to survive on.

Many hundreds of dollars were needed to continue the battle, both locally and at the appellate level. For Oliver, it was either eat or fight. He couldn't afford to do both, but the elder Saunders didn't want it to come to that. He respected Lamora's integrity and willingness to do battle in the face of overwhelming odds, and he truly believed in Oliver's cause.

To continue financing the fight, it was clear that Willard's client needed outside help. He issued an appeal for sympathizers to come forward with economic support for Lamora's case, which was, in effect, representing the rights of the public within the state-defined Adirondack Park. This was a test case, and if Lamora lost, everyone would lose.

With the help of contributions, Oliver was able to continue the court battle. The first step was to deal with the repressive injunction. At that point, Lamora was in a tenuous position.

Were he to continue fighting, he might win outright. But, if he were to lose, he faced substantial penalties, and would, in all likelihood, be forced to give up his home unless private backers decided to cover his additional costs.

With all of that in mind, Kellas and Saunders met in front of Judge Henry T. Kellogg in Malone. By mid-June they reached a tentative settlement based in part on the pending outcome of proceedings at the appellate level. All that was needed was Oliver's consent to the terms they had discussed.

Lamora understood that the law allowed for exemplary, or punitive, damages, plus costs, so the actual numbers involved were very important to him. If he fought the case and lost, he would ultimately be liable for a fine of up to $25 per violation, and would be required to pay court costs, which could be close to $1,000 by that time.

In the proposed agreement, Rockefeller consented to settle for a judgment of only six cents in damages per violation, and to pay all court costs. The catch: the terms of the injunction would be made permanent, and Lamora would agree to abide by the private park law.

Again, that settlement was only tentative. Should the appellate court decide to return the case once more to the county level, they would revert to square one on the trespassing charge. At that time, the stipulation would be enforced only if both sides concurred.

It seemed downright conciliatory to offer such "generous" financial terms, but money was never an issue with William Rockefeller. It was simply a tool. If Lamora were to take the bait and consent to the terms of the offer, he might be able to keep his home, while Rockefeller and the other wealthy owners would keep their kingdoms, forever protected by the private park law.

For Lamora personally, the risks were great. After careful consideration, he finally agreed to the stipulation, and awaited the results from the appellate level.

In July, while William Rockefeller was hosting family and friends at Bay Pond, including sons Percy and William G. and their spouses, word arrived that the appellate division had for a second time found against Lamora. And, for a second time, the trespass case had been referred back to county court for retrial.

For many, it was hard to understand the reasoning of the higher court. In spite of excellent arguments acknowledged by the justices in the first review in 1903, the court stressed that the defense had failed to prove that streams on Rockefeller property had been stocked by the state, and with the permission of the owner.

In this latest appearance before the appellate division, Willard Saunders presented clear evidence that the waters in question had been stocked by the state, and with the permission of the previous owner, Patrick Ducey.

The court accepted the evidence proving Ducey had agreed to the stocking, but took it a step further. Though Ducey owned the company and was chief financier, others had invested small amounts. Therefore, the court considered him merely "an officer" of the Ducey Lumber Company.

That conclusion produced this nugget of legal wisdom: "The individual consent of an officer of the company would not bind the corporation so as to affect the purchaser of the land."

In other words, since Ducey's consent couldn't speak for his own company, there was no consent to pass on to the new owner, William Rockefeller. The ruling seemed to give equal value to a company owner and a variety of his subordinates, something that William Rockefeller would never have accepted in his world of business and high finance. But in this case, the law was turned around to suit his needs.

To many, it appeared to be an amazing example of convoluted reasoning, similar to the court's earlier declaration that the state was, in effect, taking private property by stocking the woods with fish and game.

The issue of using public monies to raise game now being claimed by private individuals had been cast aside in deference to what the court said were property owners' rights. The Adirondack Park, a park intended for the masses, would not be an exception.

Lamora's attorney had satisfied the criteria found wanting at an earlier appearance, yet the court now decided to ignore it. But Saunders was a wily litigator, and had forged ahead with his backup plan, which addressed the issue of public highways.

He maintained that it was settled law in New York State that any trail or pathway used for twenty years or more without the consent of the owner automatically became a public highway.

From the main road through Brandon, it was those long-used trails that Lamora had traveled to access the publicly stocked waters of the Middle Branch of the St. Regis River. Therefore, he had not violated the game laws, and had not trespassed, according to Saunders.

Further, it was noted that when Mr. Rockefeller purchased the land, he had been fully aware of those established, well-worn trails used for hunting and fishing by the public.

In spite of it all, the court was not sufficiently impressed to rule against Rockefeller.

The public highway argument was being tested across the Adirondacks, and it was a great disappointment to many when the court rejected it in the Lamora trial. In some cases, the public was being denied access to hunting and fishing territory that had been used for decades, and was actually state property.

The problem was this: between certain villages and popular tracts of state land, wealthy clubs or individuals had purchased vast acreage and posted it to all trespassing. This cut off the only public access trails to the state land.

In effect, the state land became merely an addition to the private land, since nobody but the private owners could access it. And, luckily for them, it was stocked with game and fish at public expense.

New York State's own committee appointed to assess the future of the Adirondacks had come to the conclusion that the state should own the entire park for the people, and for the protection of its natural assets. Just a few months earlier, the committee had disclosed its findings, declaring, in part:

> The total acreage of the Adirondack Park as now laid out is 3,226,144 acres, of which the state owns 1,163,414 acres. The remaining acres are owned by private persons and business corporations.
>
> The committee states that ownership by the State is the most effective means of preservation, as it is easier to regulate and control its own holdings than to influence private owners to institute rational forestry methods.

With the Brandon battle returning once again to county court, the case and its adjoining issues received widespread publicity. As word filtered out that nearly a million acres of Adirondack land had already been cut off from the public, other sources of financing came forward to aid Lamora's cause.

Some donors were average Adirondack tourists, and some were wealthy visitors who did not own camps. Others felt it was simply wrong that fish and game developed for public use could become the province of a few wealthy men.

Whatever their reasons, the people spoke with their wallets. They could only hope that the court would listen. Willard Saunders certainly welcomed the backing. He hoped to prove that the wild game in the Adirondacks belonged to everyone, and that so-called preserves were transforming public property into private property, which was illegal.

Saunders planned to point out that the state had an official policy of creating an Adirondack Park for the public. Knowing this, and knowing the state did not have the funds to purchase the entire park all at once, many wealthy men and organizations had taken advantage of the situation by purchasing hundreds of thousands of prime Adirondack acreage, and then closing it off from the public.

Saunders sought to bring that practice to an end. As prominent individuals and state committees before him had recommended, he hoped the state would finally do the right thing by acting on public policy and purchasing the entire park.

The additional donations flowing in for his client's defense gave Saunders a fighting chance in the upcoming battle, but in the world of money, no voice equaled that of the Rockefellers. And, while Lamora and Saunders prepared to face their opponent head-on, they were unaware of the Rockefeller practice of attacking on multiple fronts.

With money comes power and influence, and all were at work towards the goal of eliminating Brandon from the map. While the court battle over trespassing dragged on, Rockefeller was preparing circuitous assaults intended to weaken Lamora's resolve.

As John Melin of Tarrytown could have warned him, "Watch your back." If Rockefeller didn't beat you outright, he would try to sabotage you into surrender.

In Melin's case, he wouldn't sell his business, so Rockefeller bought out all his neighbors. This eliminated Melin's customer base, and badly diminished his livelihood. Lamora wasn't running a business, so Rockefeller had to find alternatives to making life miserable for him and the remaining residents of Brandon township.

6

Tactics of War

Lamora's confinement by court injunction allowed him little contact with the outside world. His only connections were by mail and by train, and the mail in those days was dependent upon rail service. In the post-Civil War period, the United States Postal Service saw the expansion of railroads as an opportunity to provide regular, fast delivery of the mail.

Eventually, the system of Railway Mail Service (RMS) was developed, a very reliable delivery network that would remain in place for nearly a century. The arrangement became so entrenched that many rail lines stayed in business even though they were losing money on passenger service. The steady, daily job of carrying the nation's mail assured a profit.

On several occasions, Rockefeller had looked into relocating the rail line that ran through Brandon. Difficulties had surfaced involving service through the village to other locations, but he hadn't entirely abandoned the idea. It was simply on hold.

But in the mail service, he sensed a vulnerability. By Rockefeller's reasoning, if he couldn't move the rails, then perhaps he could move the mail. It followed that if there were no mail deliveries to Brandon, there would be a decreased need for rail service.

Curtailing or ending mail service to an established location was far beyond the scope of any average individual, or even most very successful men. But the Rockefellers operated on another level entirely. Wielding a little influence with Postmaster General Henry Payne was the quickest, simplest way to cut mail service to Brandon.

Rockefeller did carry with him the plausible argument that, with only a few families served at that location, it appeared that the government could consolidate services and save the taxpayers some money.

To bolster his suggestion, Rockefeller offered this cost-saving plan. The minimal work done at Brandon's post office could be performed at the Bay Pond station, where approximately sixty families were now being served, all of them Rockefeller employees. It was just a few miles down the line from Brandon, making the change a perfectly reasonable move.

Normally, such behind-the-scenes maneuvers for a man of William Rockefeller's influence would not be a problem. However, this was no ordinary time for the postal service. The department had recently experienced widely-publicized scandals on the national level, and had for some time been under investigation by the administration of Theodore Roosevelt.

Among the issues were questionable purchasing practices, and the use of influence to secure postmaster appointments and to change office locations.

A major report detailing the problems had just been issued, and a number of reforms were being implemented. Still, with a Rockefeller, the playing field never seemed to be level. In spite of the precarious situation caused by the investigation, William moved forward with his plan.

By early June 1904, he had his answer. The news was kept quiet for a while, but buried on page ten of the *New York Times* was a blurb about William Rockefeller entertaining family members at Bay Pond. Percy and William G. were there, along with John D. and Mrs. Rockefeller.

Seemingly as an afterthought, it was added that "Bay Pond has recently been made a post office, while the post office at Brandon has been abolished."

The statement was not entirely accurate, since Bay Pond's

postal branch had been in existence since December 11, 1900. However, the rest of the statement *was* correct.

According to the records of the United States Postal Department, the official decision to close Brandon's post office was made on May 31. When the ruling took effect on June 30, Postmaster Louis Strack was removed from his position, and Brandon's mail service was transferred to Bay Pond.

Brandon's post office was no more.

It would be one of Henry Payne's last official acts as postmaster general. He took ill and died in September, a few weeks after the official announcement of the Brandon-Bay Pond decision.

For William Rockefeller, there clearly was no fish too big or too small to fry. At the very same time that he had been positioning himself to rule America's railroads from coast to

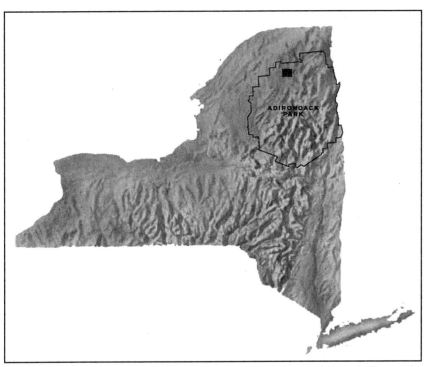

Map of New York State and the Adirondack Park. The black box indicates the location of William Rockefeller's Bay Pond Preserve.

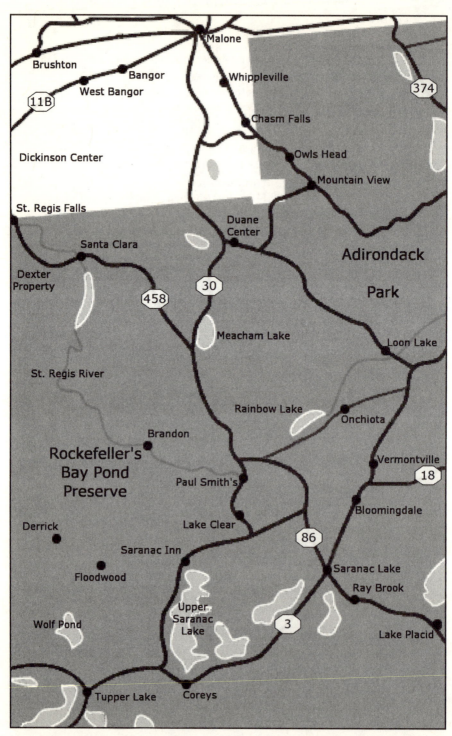

Brushton

Bangor

West Bangor

11B

Malone

Whippleville

Chasm Falls

374

Dickinson Center

Owls Head

Mountain View

St. Regis Falls

Duane Center

Santa Clara

Adirondack

Park

Dexter Property

458

30

Meacham Lake

Loon Lake

St. Regis River

Rainbow Lake

Onchiota

Brandon

Vermontville

Rockefeller's Bay Pond Preserve

Paul Smith's

18

Bloomingdale

Derrick

Lake Clear

Saranac Inn

86

Floodwood

Saranac Lake

Ray Brook

Wolf Pond

Upper Saranac Lake

3

Lake Placid

Tupper Lake

Coreys

Location of William Rockefeller's estate in the northwestern Adirondacks coast, he had also been plotting to obliterate a tiny Adirondack village by eliminating its post office.

And, while conquering the likes of the Morgans and Vanderbilts in the world of finance, he was applying similar vigor in the fight against Lamora, a poor Civil War pensioner. Unfortunately for Oliver, it was true that Rockefeller seemed to view both battles with equal importance.

The railroad issue was a high priority with Rockefeller, as it held the possibility of enormous profit for Standard Oil. After slowly gaining power through the New York Central and other railroads, William Rockefeller had just reeled in the mighty Northern Pacific, and now controlled 66,000 miles of rails.

Yet, he was still having problems controlling the fate of the railroad tracks at Brandon. Now, though, with the elimination of mail delivery, rail service might well be susceptible to the same fate.

Rockefeller's actions involving the two backwoods post offices soon became public knowledge, and the expected backlash followed. Across the Adirondacks, it was viewed as the ultimate hubris, especially when considering the events of the past year, during which Rockefeller's life had been repeatedly threatened, his camp was under virtual siege, and a similarly antagonistic figure, Orrando Dexter, had been shot dead.

In light of all that, what had William Rockefeller done? Rather than pull back to reassess the situation and the effectiveness of his tactics, he continued to attack, this time by eliminating Brandon's postal service.

The people in the town of Brandon countered by sending a petition to the Post Office Department in Washington. The signatures of more than seventy town residents graced the document, noting that many of them would be forced to travel a great distance to retrieve their mail if the office was not reinstated. There was no response from the federal level.

Rumblings of dissatisfaction from the region reached newspapers across the country. Editorials criticized Rockefeller's actions on the park issue and on the post office closure, and political ramifications were feared.

Franklin County had long been a stronghold of the

Republican Party, but public perception held that it was mostly wealthy Republicans who were greedily gobbling up Adirondack land for their own use. In doing so, they were cutting off their own constituency.

And now, the Republican administration of President Theodore Roosevelt was held responsible for closing one post office and maintaining another simply for the convenience of one wealthy family, and at the expense of scores of citizens.

Roosevelt had hoped the recent postal investigation and subsequent reforms would eliminate a very thorny issue, but the Rockefeller story garnered more negative press for the department and for his political party. There were public oaths by many northern Adirondack Republicans that they would vote for Democrats in the upcoming November elections.

To Rockefeller, none of it mattered. He didn't become one of the kings of the oil, copper, banking, and now the railroad industry by worrying about what others thought. Flush with success on the postal front, he now contemplated a variety of options regarding the rail line through Bay Pond and Brandon.

Chief among his considerations was a new take on an old idea. He proposed removing the entire rail line between Brandon and Tupper Lake.

The earlier battle between Charles Turner and the railroad owners had been won by the railroad. When Turner had resorted to hauling his logs south to the New York Central at Floodwood, he was forced to drive across the tracks of the New York & Ottawa Railroad.

To prevent this act, which they considered trespassing, the New York & Ottawa had fenced its property. Turner tore down the fence, claiming legal right-of-way, thus prompting a protracted court battle. When he lost in court, Turner closed his mill, the lifeblood of Derrick.

As a result, there was very little rail traffic left between Brandon and Derrick, both of which appeared to be headed towards extinction. And William Rockefeller could not have been more pleased.

Rockefeller suggested running the line at St. Regis Falls southeast towards Lake Clear, but completely avoiding Brandon and Bay Pond. From Lake Clear, Tupper Lake would still be accessible by the rails of the New York Central.

Then, the tracks between Brandon and Tupper Lake could be torn up, and Rockefeller would have his privacy at last.

As word of Rockefeller's removal of the post office gained notice, along with his continued assault on Brandon's existence, the feelings of hatred in the Adirondacks were heightened. Wealthy landowners were demonized, and there was a renewed surge of public opinion against the existence of private parks. It seemed as if the turmoil would never end.

It had now been a year since Orrando Dexter had been shot dead. No arrest had been made, and the crime was still being investigated. Henry Dexter, father of the deceased, pressed on in his hunt for the killer.

Attorney Azro Blake, who had worked for Orrando, continued to toil on behalf of the elder Dexter, but he had been harassed constantly as he sought to determine the identity of the murderer.

The intensity of feelings across the region caused Blake to temporarily give up the chase. He articulated his reasons in a letter to Henry Dexter:

> I have left Nicholville, near Lake Dexter, for
> Massena [twenty miles north]. I think a change will
> make me feel more easy. During the investigation
> of your son's murder, I awoke one morning to find
> a big red splash of blood high up on my door. The
> warning was too clear to be mistaken and, although
> I always go armed, I cannot shake off a creepy
> sensation.

Besides Blake, there were several New York City detectives still on the case, hired by William Rockefeller. They, too, were frequently threatened by locals, some of whom felt strongly in favor of retaining their old way of life. Others wouldn't talk to the detectives, fearing repercussions if they were perceived as being cooperative with the enemy.

The situation continued to deteriorate, which unfortunately brought more negative publicity. The story of Rockefeller's battle to wipe out Brandon received coverage from Montreal to Winnipeg, from Maine to California, from Oregon to Florida.

Though it was not always accurately depicted, readers were regaled with the tale of a financial colossus fairly obsessed with obliterating a tiny mountain community and crushing the spirit of its lone defender, a poor but determined Civil War veteran. It made for great theater, but for folks in the northern Adirondacks, the story was all too real.

Perhaps William Rockefeller had gone too far this time. Had he overestimated his ability to drive the people out? After all, his assaults on Brandon had taken many forms, but the struggle was still ongoing.

He had wiped out every business in the village except for Joe Peryea's small hotel and store. He had reduced the population to near zero, destroyed many of the buildings, and restricted access to all of the surrounding forest and roads.

He had removed the village post office and was constantly seeking ways to eliminate rail service. He had taken many locals to court on charges of trespassing, illegal hunting, and illegal fishing. And, he had thoroughly antagonized much of the region with his callous treatment of Brandon's citizens.

Public sympathies were clearly on the side of Lamora and his fellow rebels, but that mattered little to William Rockefeller. No Rockefeller had ever won a popularity contest, and William was sure to maintain that tradition.

Rockefeller's actions so infuriated people that many of them persisted in striking back, even at their own peril. Trespassing remained a frequent offense, entailing the risk of attack by preserve guards, and the painful reality of court-imposed fines.

Occasionally the confrontations between trespassers and Rockefeller guards became physical. Then, things escalated, as feelings boiled over, and weapons were used. Several times, shots were fired in the direction of the preserve keepers.

In one instance, widespread headlines introduced readers to the story of a guard who had been fired upon. It was reported that a bullet passed through his coat sleeve, whereupon he retired from the Rockefeller guard force.

Adding to the maelstrom was a threatening letter received

by Henry Dexter regarding his son's murder. Events had taken an ugly twist, and Dexter released the letter's contents to the press, generating the following story:

> What is believed to be another clue to the murder of Orrando P. Dexter, who was shot down from ambush at Lake Dexter, in the Adirondacks, was given to Henry Dexter, the millionaire publisher, at his home, says a New York dispatch. It came in a letter dated in Newark and mailed in New York at 7 o'clock Wednesday morning.
>
> The letter, apparently by design, had been put in an illiterate form to give the appearance of the work of a hunter or back-woodsman. The words were put into printed form to conceal the handwriting of the writer.
>
> It reads as follows: "I shot your son and I am glad of it. He put me away from his fishing place and I put him to death. You can get the gun that was fired in such rapidness and hit the mark, about two miles from the place he was shot, in line with Boonville.
>
> "I tried the window game, but I could not get what I wanted. I knew the cook saw me and I walked away. I will confess when I am ready to die. If I thought I could get the old man I would get up for deer this season. One innocent has paid his life for my crime and others unsolved. The old man wants lynch law, but I say lead for the likes of his son."
>
> The suggestion as to the location of the gun and what the cook saw will be investigated by Mr. Dexter's lawyers and agents, in the hope that something may be found to clear up the mystery. Mr. Dexter's secretary said that the identity of the man who shot Mr. Dexter was known, and legal evidence was being sought to place before the grand jury to substantiate the charge of homicide.

With violence and threats forming the backdrop, the next phase of the Rockefeller-Lamora court battle was fast approaching. Other wealthy industrialists were busy lobbying state officials on behalf of Rockefeller, and he did reap some support from a few locals whose publicized letters supported the removal of Brandon's post office, since it was doing minimal business, no matter what the reason.

There was also some backing from people who felt that Rockefeller was merely exercising his rights as a property owner, like any other individual was entitled to do. That argument was countered by those who noted it was state policy to preserve the Adirondack land within the Blue Line as a vast public park for all of its citizens.

It was the same policy that Rockefeller had spoken in favor of many times in the past, while at the same time purchasing nearly 80,000 acres of that very land and sealing it off for his own personal use.

For the most part, public support was behind both Lamora's fight and the effort to eliminate the private park law, since park ownership was possible only for a very few citizens in the entire country. But public opinion doesn't always dictate government policy, and money often does. Few lobbyists spoke on behalf of the common man.

By this time, despite the donations from several New York City sportsmen, Lamora's funds were running dry. He had little of value in the world except for his Brandon home. Willard Saunders truly believed in Oliver's fight, and to further support his cause, he granted the old man a $900 mortgage on his Brandon property.

Lamora had help from other quarters, too. In hopes of bolstering the upcoming court case, a guide from the Tupper Lake area, Fred McNeil, told reporters that he had recently covered all of the trails in the vicinity of Buck Mountain and Brandon.

In his travels, he had visited nearly a dozen bodies of water, including Bay Pond, and had walked the shores of the St. Regis River. All of the locations mentioned were on the Rockefeller preserve.

McNeil pointed out that this was the eighteenth consecutive year that he had walked the trails of that region, maintaining the status of those paths as public highways. He made the trek in mid-November and hoped the court would take his efforts into consideration when Lamora's case was argued.

Finally, the day of reckoning arrived, and on Friday, December 16, the two sides faced off in Franklin County court. This marked the third consecutive December during which the Rockefeller-Lamora case was tried in the same venue.

The immediate issue was the charge of trespassing, but arguments were certain to digress into several related issues, including the legality of private parks.

Through Friday and most of Saturday, the trial continued, but little new information was proffered by either side. After all, the issue had already been before every court in the state, and at least twice at each level.

Lamora could have opted to accept the terms of the stipulation that had been worked out earlier, but he chose to fight on. Judge Beman, having now heard the case for the third time in three years, decided it was time to end it.

In front of Beman in 1902, Rockefeller's action had been "non-suited" by the jury, meaning that, after hearing the plaintiff's evidence, they determined that there were no grounds for a lawsuit.

In 1903, the jury had found "no cause of action," which was basically the same as the "non-suited" finding. Both times, the case had gone before the state appellate court and had been returned to the county level.

In light of those appearances, and in consideration of the previous rulings of the higher court, Judge Beman ended the proceedings with a directed verdict.

A directed verdict (and its modern counterpart, "judgment as a matter of law") relieves the jury of the decision-making process in terms of finding for the plaintiff or the defendant.

Instead, the judge makes that decision, and the jury then determines the damages, if any. Though Lamora had won three times before a justice of the peace and twice before juries at the county court level, Judge Beman followed the appellate court decisions and found in favor of Rockefeller.

The jury met for only five minutes, announcing an award of

damages to Rockefeller in the sum of six cents for each infraction, for a total of eighteen cents.

Though the damages were nominal, the jury also awarded costs, which meant that Lamora would be saddled with a hefty fee for expenses after having battled in county court three times and at the appellate level twice.

In hopes of ending the case once and for all, Judge Beman fired one final volley, denying a motion by the defense for a new trial.

Willard Saunders planned to appeal the decision at the state level, but thus far, the higher court had not been sympathetic to his arguments on behalf of Lamora. The outcome seemed predetermined.

To Oliver and like-minded people of the north, this was devastating news. The private parks were now protected by law, and natives knew it was the end of an era. Never again could men choose to roam free in the Adirondack wilderness, extracting a living from what nature supplied in abundance.

Rockefeller's victory received press attention across the nation, but it wasn't trumpeted as a great conquest. Instead, the primary headlines seemed to delight in pointing out that Rockefeller (with an estimated worth of $100 million) had won such a trivial financial award.

Among the favorites were "Rockefeller Enriched By Eighteen Cents" and "Millionaire Gets Eighteen Cents Damages."

The secondary headlines touted the great resistance offered by Lamora, the simple, hardy, mountain man, defending with all his might the pioneer way of life. Again, a quaint, poignant story, but with the poorer man ultimately losing. For Oliver, it was tough to accept.

Judge Beman's decision was decried from many sources, and for many reasons. It was very damaging to those across the region who wanted the state to give the people the park it had promised them.

Plus, there were cries of foul play, since the jury had been removed from the decision-making process. Though Beman's resolution of the case was an accepted legal maneuver, the directed verdict in favor of Rockefeller only served to reinforce the public perception that big money always wins.

State officials were lobbied to change the private park law, and to exercise eminent domain proceedings in order to make the land available to all. A provision for just that purpose had been included in the park law, but was seldom used.

The court's decision provided fodder for another source of great criticism of Rockefeller, this time based in the readership of *Collier's* magazine. Publishing partner Robert Collier frequented the Raquette Lake area of the Adirondacks, where his family had a camp, and was well aware of the goings-on up north.

Noted investigative journalist Samuel H. Adams wrote a feature story for *Collier's*, relating the story of Brandon and its fight to remain a village. Some of Rockefeller's odious tactics were exposed, and newspapers picked up bits of the story.

Particularly revealing in the magazine's exposé was a story detailing the departure of Harrison Baker, a noted hotel operator and Brandon village leader. Earlier, Baker's move had been portrayed as a gracious parting on the best of terms.

But Adams reported that Baker had been warned by Rockefeller's men he would have to sell his property and leave the village, or they would wipe out his business.

Until that time, Baker's hotel had been very successful, and he had no intentions of leaving. But, as Rockefeller purchased more property and posted it, Baker's business plummeted. He was told that he and his patrons would not be allowed to cross Rockefeller's property to reach the banks of the St. Regis River for fishing, and that they would be arrested if they hunted in his woods.

For Baker, there was no voluntary departure from Brandon. His business had been ruined, and he was forced to sell out. His story was just one of many similar tales. As brother J.D. had often done, William had used the tools of the corporate bully to get what he wanted.

Other attacks were leveled at Rockefeller for his membership in organizations sworn to preserve and protect the northern forests. One such group, the Association for the Protection of the Adirondacks, was led by several of America's wealthiest businessmen.

Among Rockefeller's fellow trustees were J.P. Morgan, Harry Payne Whitney, and Alfred G. Vanderbilt. A group like that carried plenty of clout in any arena.

A mission statement issued two years earlier by the association received replay in the press:

> We regard the Adirondack Park, with its forests, waters, and fauna, as one of Nature's legacies to our State, which the dictates of prudence, wise public policy, and foresight, require should be carefully safeguarded and protected, not only as a pleasure ground, but as conservator of the water supply for our rivers and canals. We therefore favor resumption by the State of the purchase of lands within the limits of the Adirondack Park.

It might well have been more honest and accurate to state *our* pleasure ground instead of *a* pleasure ground. After all, the Adirondacks had already long been both home and playground to mountain residents, who were now being pushed aside.

The association had clarified its intent in 1904 regarding preservation of the forests, again encouraging the state to purchase more land, but with certain priorities in mind. It urged the acquisition of all denuded lands first, the tracts that had been clear-cut by ruthless logging companies.

The association added that private preserves and club holdings should be at the bottom of the purchase list of desirable properties, to be considered only after all other possibilities had been exhausted. Those were of lowest importance for the state to acquire, the argument went, because they were already well protected (usually by association members).

No mention was made of the fact that those were also the most desirable properties for public enjoyment, yet were set aside for private use only. To the general public, such claims of "protecting" the land rang hollow.

The outcry generated by both the Lamora decision and the perceived insensitivity and greed of several estate owners continued unabated. As for William Rockefeller, he always seemed to find a way of rubbing salt in the wound. Shortly after the court ruled in his favor, he expanded his private preserve by purchasing an additional 1,240 acres of land.

In spite of the setbacks they had been dealt, there was a bit of good news for Lamora and the few remaining citizens of Brandon. The public outcry, the negative press, and the complaints about the closure of Brandon's post office had been heard. The combined effect of those efforts had resulted in an embarrassed about-face by the Post Office Department.

The petitioned request had been revisited, and on January 26, 1905, Louis Strack was reinstated as Brandon's postmaster.

Fourth Assistant Postmaster General James Bristow had done a thorough job investigating wrongdoings at all levels in the postal system, and his efforts were key in getting the Brandon office restored.

In fact, Bristow was too thorough for his own good. Pressure from those fighting the federal investigation led to Bristow's reassignment even before the Brandon move was announced.

The change came about through an executive order from the president's desk. To avoid the appearance of bending to wealthy special interests, President Roosevelt characterized Bristow's new role as a promotion.

Bristow was named commissioner of the investigation into trade relations connected to the canal and railroad in Panama. His departure would prove significant to the efficiency and honesty of postal operations in the coming year.

Amidst the uproar in early 1905, Willard Saunders petitioned the appellate court to review Judge Beman's findings. After losing on the trespassing charge, Oliver had since been billed $790.31 for court costs. If nothing else, perhaps that amount would be reduced or eliminated by the findings of the upper court.

Atop the appellate division was the New York State Court of Appeals, representing one last chance for Oliver to win. That's where Saunders hoped to land the case. Once the court of appeals made a ruling, no further venues remained, and the case would be closed.

During this period, the Adirondacks were in turmoil. Newspapers at all levels featured letters, editorials, and articles arguing the merits of each case. Some were civil and polite, while others were filled with bitterness and vitriol.

Henry Dexter, now ninety-three years old and still deeply involved in the search for his son's killer, disclosed in an interview that a recent attempt had been made on the life of one of Rockefeller's estate managers. He reported that the man had been fired upon, the bullet grazing his scalp and leaving a flesh wound.

Added Dexter:

> They murdered my son up there, and they will murder more if they have a chance. They regard all newcomers who are wealthy as interlopers and tyrants who have bought up the lands. The murderers are ignorant natives who have fanatical views opposed to wealth.
>
> I am satisfied that it would be unsafe for William Rockefeller to visit his estate this summer. Soon after my son's murder, a newspaper clipping was sent to me, on the margin of which was written the following words: "Good job, well done. A few more like it will be the best thing this country could have happen to it. William Rockefeller next, the wretch, and a dozen more such, and this country will be rid of the most dangerous element."
>
> I am not surprised to hear that threats are again being made. I sold the Dexter preserves in Franklin and St. Lawrence counties soon after my son's death.

In the mountains of far northern New York, it was hoped by many that the harsh words and threats against Rockefeller were merely venting, or bravado. No one wanted a repeat of the Dexter incident, but the talk at train stations, barbershops, and watering holes was very disturbing.

Then, in late May, bold, spectacular headlines shouted to the world that the Adirondack natives had threatened to kill William Rockefeller.

Because of his dogged pursuit of Brandon village and Oliver Lamora's property, and his continued hunt for Dexter's killer, Rockefeller risked taking a bullet if he came back to the Adirondacks.

A number of signs to that effect had been found posted along the railroad to Bay Pond and on Rockefeller's estate. They stated simply, "A $50,000 bullet will stop Mr. Rockefeller the moment he steps upon these grounds."

Reporters in New York City spoke with Rockefeller's son, William G., who discounted the admonitions and assured them his father would not be intimidated:

> Young William Rockefeller does not take seriously the sensational stories of threats lately published. He laughed at the tale of strings of bullets said to have been hung on the door of the Rockefeller lodge, and other mystic portents of revenge, declaring that his father would go to the Adirondacks as usual, and that he had not the slightest intention of selling his estate there, such a thought never having entered his mind.
>
> "Now, as for the alleged threats against my father," said he, "they are really not worth serious consideration. As a matter of fact, I do not believe they were ever made. If they had been, I would have known it, for I am in constant communication with the supervisors of the estate at Bay Pond."

In light of the Dexter murder and the hard feelings that existed at Brandon and across the Adirondacks, Rockefeller knew, of course, that there *was* danger in going to Bay Pond. His presence alone might stir things up even worse. He never backed down from a fight, but he certainly didn't want to end up like poor Dexter.

It appeared from all angles that it would be best if William were to step away from the limelight for a while. In a sense, that's what he did.

William Rockefeller had other problems brewing on a much larger scale. The rising national tide of outrage against the practices of the Standard Oil Trust had prompted action on several fronts. The government had conducted hearings and

As these articles from 1905 reveal, when death threats were made against William Rockefeller of Standard Oil fame, reporters had a field day. A hundred years ago, there was no television and no radio, making it difficult to gain modern perspective when considering major stories of years past.

Newspapers were the only wide-ranging news source. Despite that fact, one consistency over the years remains true in America: the major media consider the President of the United States as the most newsworthy individual.

In the early 1900s, that was the same type of coverage afforded the Rockefeller family. Often, even the slightest Rockefeller endeavor soon became front-page material. The great interest in everything Rockefeller helped make the names Lamora and Brandon familiar to readers across the country for a decade.

Page 1 - The Washington Post

Rockefeller Threatened

Signs Warn Millionaire He Will Be Slain if He Visits His Estate

Special to The Washington Post

May 22 – William Rockefeller, the Standard Oil magnate, who owns a magnificent preserve at Bay Pond, in the Adirondacks, has been threatened with assassination if he visits his estate the coming summer. Within the past few weeks there have been posted on trees within the Rockefeller preserve roughly printed signs which read, "A $50,000 bullet will stop Mr. Rockefeller the moment he steps upon these grounds."

As many as thirty such signs have been discovered, all evidently painted by the same persons. Among Adirondack woodsmen there is no attempt to disguise the feeling against Mr. Rockefeller. Every act of his in recent years has increased the hatred against him on the part of the natives. Several lawsuits for trespassing have heightened this feeling, which primarily is due to his treatment of the people in the location of a post office, which was removed from Brandon to Bay Pond some time ago, and the further fact that he is alleged to have displayed great activity in trying to run down the murderer of Orrando P. Dexter over a year ago.

A BULLET FOR A ROCKEFELLER

Adirondack Natives Post Threat to Kill About Rich Man's Estate

May 23 – William Rockefeller, the multimillionaire Standard Oil magnate, who owns 150 square miles of the Adirondack forest lands, has been threatened with death. A notice posted on trees throughout his domain reads:

> A $50,000 bullet will stop William Rockefeller the minute he steps foot on this property.

It is supposed that the writer of the threat is some person who has either suffered by the millionaire's policy of acquiring every acre of land he can secure by methods which are considered piratical by the old-time settlers, or by some person or persons whom Mr. Rockefeller has been pursuing since the mysterious murder of Orrando P. Dexter. It was in this very neighborhood, in September 1903, that Dexter, a wealthy New York landholder, was shot and killed. Both men obtained great tracts of land, and to protect their game and fish preserves, attempted to drive out the native woodsmen. Several New York detectives who were on the case left only when threatened with death.

Page 1 - The Post-Standard, Syracuse

STRING OF BULLETS TO WARN ROCKEFELLER
Stories That the Life of the Magnate Has Been Threatened

Malone, May 22 – A string of bullets found hanging to the door knob of the residence of William Rockefeller at Bay Pond has started all sorts of rumors about threats on the life of the Standard Oil magnate.

The story was sent out that on trees along the line of the New York & Ottawa Railroad were posted this ominous warning: "A $50,000 bullet will stop William Rockefeller the minute he sets foot on this property."

The hatred of Rockefeller is due to his treatment of the people of the village of Brandon, near his 150 square miles of hunting and fishing ground. The prosecution of trespassers has also aroused the indignation of the people against him.

ordered an investigation, and some states made similar moves on their own.

Legislators and many businessmen were anxious to get the Rockefeller brothers and their cohorts into the witness chair. The main targets were the presumed masterminds of the trust: J.D. Rockefeller, William Rockefeller, and Henry H. Rogers.

Of all the principals involved, William Rockefeller was the most reluctant to testify. He knew that a government representative first had to serve him with a subpoena, and he resolved to stay one step ahead of the feds.

Hiding out in his secure Adirondack retreat would have been perfect, but there were those nasty death threats against him. So, William decided to leave the country. As Rogers, J.D., and even son William G. faced possible court summons', William Rockefeller slipped quietly off to Europe.

While overseas, he cabled all necessary instructions to his Adirondack, Tarrytown, and New York City homes. Any hands-on work deemed necessary was delegated to his son, William G.

The Lamora issue was still a bothersome one for Rockefeller, especially considering the great uproar it had recently caused. It certainly seemed best to just let the furor subside for a time. Instead, it was about to escalate.

Less than two months after the threats against Rockefeller had been posted on his estate, a Brandon resident was arrested for taking deer out of season. His name: Oliver Lamora.

It seems that Eugene Flanders, game manager on Rockefeller's preserve, somehow discovered that Lamora had in his possession a quantity of venison. No one indicated how Flanders came by this knowledge, but he passed the information on to George Selkirk, a New York State Game Protector.

Since it was early August and hunting season was not yet open, it was illegal to possess venison. Selkirk went to Brandon to investigate. He searched Lamora's property, and in the cellar, in a pork barrel, he found the carcass of a deer. (A pork barrel was a barrel of brine water used in the process of preserving meat before the days of refrigeration.)

There was still hair on the meat, so it was clearly a recent kill. Lamora was charged with possession of venison during the closed hunting season.

Lamora claimed that the carcass wasn't his, and that some of his enemies had put the deer there to effect his arrest. But, considering the physical evidence before him, Selkirk filed charges, which carried a penalty of $100 upon conviction.

Lamora went to Willard Saunders, explained what had transpired, and claimed he had been framed by Rockefeller's men. The argument did appear to have some credence.

Flanders had been placed by Rockefeller in the building directly across the street from Lamora's house, and Oliver had assumed Flanders was put there to keep watch on both him and the Peryea clan. By that time, there were barely a dozen families left in the village, and perhaps thirty homes still standing. About 300 others had been leveled and burned.

Since Lamora suspected he was the focus of Flanders' efforts, it appeared unlikely he would risk bringing an illegal deer into his home. It seemed he had too much at stake, and it was doubtful that he would jeopardize all he had worked for by committing such a reckless act.

Oliver's only neighbors were a few anti-Rockefeller holdouts, and it was not even credible to consider that one of them might have supplied the information against Lamora if he had taken a deer illegally.

It was possible that Oliver was, in fact, guilty, based on his rebel attitude, but since his intentional trespassing in early 1902, he had steered clear of trouble for more than three years. There was a suspicion that the charges were phony, and that Rockefeller himself was behind the whole thing. But William was in faraway Europe, safely distanced from the controversy.

The case was brought before Judge Marsha of Tupper Lake, but due to the peripheral issues that might be involved, it was rescheduled for Franklin County Supreme Court action.

As the months passed, Oliver's case did not appear on the court calendar. It seemed that Rockefeller might be content to let the issue lie idle for a time, perhaps until the court rendered its final ruling on the appeal of Judge Beman's decision.

In October, Willard Saunders delivered news to Oliver about his original case. The appellate division had upheld Judge

Beman's ruling, but had granted Sanders' request for the case to be brought to the court of appeals. The final decision was now in the hands of the state's highest court.

The gravity of the case was reinforced by a lengthy commentary appearing in *Forest and Stream*, where the editors weighed in on the various issues. Years earlier, the magazine had taken the stance that private parks, though controversial, had helped deer and other wildlife recover from the devastation by unscrupulous lumbermen and so-called sportsmen.

Now, the writers warned about the dangers of the parks, and the true importance of Rockefeller versus Lamora:

> This case is unquestionably the greatest case involving game preserves ever tried in America, and on its final result hangs the fate of the efforts to establish 'parks' in the Adirondack wild land after the English 'farm and preserve' system. In the Adirondacks, the preserves are engaged in lumbering, while in England, agriculture, etc., is followed.
>
> The real defendant in the matter is the public. Rockefeller is not trying to defend himself from aggressions on his rights, but he is suing a man who followed a public highway to a stream of water to which the public has as much right as to the air they breathe, and caught trout which Rockefeller did not plant, but some of which the State did plant, and the rest of which were propagated naturally, and under circumstances, and in waters which made them unquestionably public property.
>
> The broad, undeniable principle for which Saunders has been fighting is this: Time and again the courts, legislatures, and juries have held that wild game, wild fish, and wild birds belong to the people. If Rockefeller finally wins this case, he, a private individual, will receive from Oliver LaMora, exemplary damages because LaMora caught public trout out of public waters reached from a public highway.
>
> The suit is not for trespass under the common law; it is for damages under the Private Park Law,

so-called. And it is held by the defense that this Private Park law is unconstitutional because it takes public property from the people and puts it into the possession of private individuals without the consent of the required two-thirds vote of the Legislature and the vote of the people.

It is a principle, long established in law and custom, and now admitted by the Appellate Division that wild game, wild fish, and wild birds belong to the public. The courts have held this to be so repeatedly, but William Rockefeller's case against Oliver LaMora is a fight to break down this oft-repeated principle.

The case has got far beyond a mere justice's court suit between a land holder and a poacher. It is now a question of how much a man of vast wealth and tremendous influence can take from the public. It remains to be seen whether Mr. Rockefeller can get the very birds of the air, and the fish of the waters, and the mammals of the land into his possession, as he has gotten the lands.

The next step is the one before the highest court in the State, by which it will be decided whether or not Rockefeller has the right to exact a penalty from people who catch trout from streams on his lands. If Mr. Rockefeller wins, the cause of private parks will receive an aid, without which they cannot exist.

And at the same time, the people will be deprived of their rights in the fish, game, and birds on more than 700,000 acres of Adirondack forest lands. The LaMora case is not an action for mere trespass; it is one to secure a penalty for trout caught, and those trout are public property, according to laws and opinions reaching back to the days of old England.

Willard Saunders, in part due to the attention gained by resourcefully handling Lamora's and similar trespassing cases, had been recently selected as the Democratic Party candidate for assembly in the upcoming elections. His chances of winning were minimal, though, for the area had long been a bulwark of Republicanism.

From the *Chateaugay Record and Franklin County Democrat*, the following is a partisan commentary supporting Saunders' candidacy, rendered here for its simplicity in stating the Rockefeller-Lamora issues:

> Those who believe in the preservation of any vestige of popular rights in the Adirondacks cannot help admiring Mr. Saunders for the sturdy struggle he has made in defending poor old Lamora from the persecutions of Rockefeller.
>
> Law abiding as we may be, ready as we are to recognize the right of Rockefeller to exclude everybody else from the earth after he has bought it, we cannot help sympathizing with the poor old fellow who is being 'pushed off into the sea.'
>
> Great as is our respect for property rights, we can have only disgust for the man who would prefer to see wild berries rot by the wayside rather than see some hungry child eat them, and who piles up and burns the rubbish from his demolished buildings at an expense to himself, rather than let some poor person enjoy it for fuel.
>
> The Jewish code provided that the harvesters must leave some scatterings on the ground to satisfy the necessities of the poor gleaners. Rockefeller would make the ground barren so that the inhabitants must flee from his sight.
>
> If Mr. Saunders shall be elected to the Assembly, we believe some effort will be made to amend the laws so as to compel Rockefeller to pay some of the taxes he now evades by claiming a home in Franklin County.

The statement did reflect the fact that not everyone was bitter against Rockefeller, but it was disheartening that he had shown so little respect for the people he was displacing, treating them as if they were cattle to be moved to another field.

Since his arrival in the northern mountains, Rockefeller had exhibited a general disregard for all except those who agreed to work for him. He could endure those employees living on his estate at Bay Pond, but could not tolerate the residents who remained at Brandon.

There was one defining difference between the two groups. The people at Brandon were not under his control.

Late in 1905, government efforts to locate William Rockefeller in relation to the Standard Oil hearings proved fruitless. In October, William G. handled the duties of family spokesman by providing a statement to the press. He revealed that his father had gone overseas several months earlier under the advice of his physicians, and that he may not be returning for some time yet.

Said William G.: "The physicians prescribed a long rest for my father, and advised him not to hurry his return. No, there is nothing seriously wrong with him, but he has been in need of an extended rest for a long time."

The convenient timing of the previously undisclosed illness and lengthy recovery period was not lost on the press. And, Rockefeller turned out to be correct in his assumption that subpoenas were on the way. Shortly after William G.'s statement, he was served with a summons in the case of Missouri versus Standard Oil. Many more subpoenas would follow.

While William was off to Europe, leaving behind death threats and court-ordered appearances, the hoped-for calming never developed at his Adirondack estate, where family members were busy entertaining guests.

Feelings were still running high, and with hunting season in full swing, it didn't help matters when newspapers featured stories of Mrs. William Rockefeller bagging the biggest buck of the season, while fifty armed guards patrolled the preserve grounds.

For hunters who once frequented those woods, but were now forbidden to enter, it was galling to read of her exploits. Again, more salt in the wound.

7

Oliver Strikes Back

During that winter season, the Rockefellers weren't the only ones entertaining visitors. Guests of a different sort arrived in Brandon in January 1906. A state forestry official had been sent to investigate claims of illegal cutting on some wooded tracts of state land in the area. He was accompanied by a surveyor, and together they stayed at Oliver Lamora's place for three weeks.

Rockefeller owned most of the land surrounding Brandon, and it was believed to be his loggers who had wandered onto state land and cut a stand of timber. Of course, suspicion as to the identity of the informant was focused on Oliver, especially since he hosted the investigators. The irony was obvious: Lamora behind charges of trespass against Rockefeller.

At any rate, the forestry official, William H. King, determined that the state border had been breached by more than three hundred feet, but the perpetrator was not named. It was ordered that all cut logs be left where they lay.

Whether or not there was any connection, a few weeks later Rockefeller shut down the entire logging operation he had been conducting on the Debar Mountain tract, which up to that time had yielded a huge amount of timber. The closing had a sense of permanence about it, as plans were made to remove the four-mile railroad spur that connected the logging camp with the line of the New York Central.

The trespass story was trivial compared to what came next. In March, international headlines shouted, "Rockefeller Dying!" The story that followed told how William Rockefeller was suffering from stomach cancer. In part, the reports said:

> He has lived under tremendous strain for forty years. He has been the speculative member of the Standard group of capitalists, and has engineered all of the vast deals of that combination in the stock market. Next to his elder brother, he is probably the richest man in the United States. The illness of William Rockefeller is a blow of stupendous proportions to the Standard Oil group.

The story went on to tell how the family had gone to great lengths to conceal his incurable affliction, and how cancer of the stomach "causes the most excruciating agony to its victims."

The news stunned the financial world, as William had become even more powerful with the recent "semi-retirement" of his brother, J.D. What would become of mighty Standard Oil? Would the news help quell the furor in the Adirondacks?

The story was allowed to play through the press for four days. Then, amidst all the concern and speculation, son William G. issued a statement that was no less shocking than the original announcement. (Note the interesting similarity of the first line to the famous quote attributed to Mark Twain in 1897, "Reports of my death are greatly exaggerated." Twain was a very close friend of Rockefeller's Standard Oil partner Henry Rogers.)

Said William G. to the *Washington Post*:

> The reports about my father's condition have been greatly exaggerated. There is not a word of truth in the statement that he is suffering from a cancer. The real cause of his illness was a nervous breakdown. It may take some months, but he is sure to come out all right.

It was an astounding turnabout. Had it been a ploy, a story planted to perhaps gain sympathy for William in the face of the building sentiment against Standard Oil?

If so, it had little chance of working. His brother, J.D., was continuously vilified in the press even as he gave away many millions of dollars. With the path they had taken to riches, sympathy for either of the Rockefellers was out of the question.

Whatever or whomever was behind the story, William would have had to wait a long time to receive any condolences from the Adirondacks, especially in the far north. The media was still filled with all sorts of commentary against the private parks, with no letup in sight.

The earlier announcement of William Rockefeller's illness coincided with the release of the March 1906 issue of *Forest and Stream*, in which editor Perry Fraser offered a detailed assessment of the situation in the Adirondacks.

He had just accompanied Chief Game Protector John Burnham on an extended trek of more than one hundred miles through the region, most of it on snowshoes.

Said Fraser:

> As far as enjoyment by the public of the parks is concerned, such parks as William Rockefeller's, for instance, are decidedly more of a menace than fire and ax.
>
> In addition to his eighty square miles in his Brandon and Bay Pond tract, Mr. Rockefeller is said to own in the Everton, Meacham Lake, and Debar Mountain and other contiguous or nearly contiguous tracts, an even larger extent of land, and it is commonly stated that he owns or holds an option on 200,000 acres, or over 300 square miles of Adirondack lands, from which the public is or will be excluded.
>
> It is true that in numerous instances the private parks afford shelter and breeding grounds for deer, which overflow and help to keep up the supply in the surrounding territory, but many of the owners of parks are influenced solely by materialistic motives, and strip their lands wherever they can make a profit. Rockefeller, for example, has been in the market a good deal of recent years as a seller of stumpage,

and most of the paper and pulp companies post their lands under the private park law.

The only hope for the general public, if not for the deer supply, is therefore in the State ownership of Adirondack lands. It is the one and only resource to prevent the reckless waste of the forests and to preserve for the people the opportunity for rest and recreation afforded by their priceless wilderness heritage.

While the park issue was debated in the press in early 1906, the action at Brandon had taken on a whole new twist. The Forest, Fish, and Game Commission had once again received reports of game law violations on the Bay Pond estate of William Rockefeller. So, what was new?

Here's what was new: the two accused violators were Rockefeller's own estate superintendent and his primary gamekeeper. This was indeed a jaw-dropping revelation.

The commission had been informed that fox hounds were kept on the Rockefeller estate, and that they were being used to hunt deer. Not only was hounding illegal, but deer season had closed months earlier, in mid-November.

John Burnham, the state's Chief Game Protector, was sent to investigate the veracity of the claims. Burnham took the charges seriously, and he arrived unannounced at Bay Pond in hopes of catching the perpetrators in action.

For several days in March, Burnham used snowshoes to track the hunters across Rockefeller's estate. By week's end, he had seen all he needed to see.

At Dickinson Center, about twenty miles northwest of Bay Pond, Burnham held a court of inquiry, where it was determined that the men on the preserve had been keeping and using fox hounds. This was in clear violation of the game law, since all dogs capable of running deer were prohibited from the forest.

Burnham indicated he expected to file charges against both Rockefeller employees for keeping hounds illegally, and for hounding deer.

One can only imagine the glee experienced by Lamora's supporters. While they and Oliver had been chased from the woods, the fox had been left guarding the henhouse!

The men involved were two of the chief pursuers of Lamora: Bay Pond Superintendent John Redwood, and Harry Melville, a Rockefeller gamekeeper. Even more embarrassing was the fact that Redwood had been reappointed four months earlier as a deputy sheriff, an actual officer of the law.

A trial was held before Justice Horace Hazen at Dickinson Center. The state's case was presented by Deputy Attorney General Hamilton Ward Jr., who served as special counsel to the game commission. Ward had gained a reputation for aggressive prosecution of timber and game violations. His successes had prompted warnings and even death threats against him, but he refused to be intimidated.

Before going to court, Ward had to deal with William G., who was handling matters for his father while the elder Rockefeller was in Europe. The younger William hoped his influence would bring about some type of pre-trial settlement, but Ward wouldn't waver from the original charges.

Facing a hostile team of Rockefeller attorneys, Ward proved that Redwood had "three deer hounds" at Bay Pond. The evidence supplied by Burnham confirmed that not only did they have the dogs on the preserve, but they had used them to hunt deer. Lawyers for the defense claimed that the dogs were fox hounds, and had only been used to hunt foxes.

Both Melville and Redwood were convicted of keeping dogs in the State Forest Preserve, and for hounding deer. A fine of $100 was imposed on each man. It was a great public humiliation for Rockefeller, and all preserve owners indirectly, to be caught red-handed on private park land which had been established for the "protection and propagation of game."

William G.'s men had an ominous warning of their own for Ward as the trial ended. The attorney was told he would soon be practicing law in another part of the state. But Ward stood firm, as did Attorney General Julius Mayer behind him. The Rockefeller side filed an appeal, moving the case to Franklin County court.

For William G., this was another problem he could have done without. He was already facing court action in several

How powerful was William Rockefeller, Oliver Lamora's adversary? Far beyond anyone who exists today in the world of business. With older brother John D. still involved, but semi-retired, William was at the top.

Consider this. When the Standard Oil Trust was eventually forced by the government to disperse, it was broken into thirty-five companies. Remember years ago when gas stations dotted the landscape, marked prominently by signs for Amoco, Chevron, Conoco, Exxon, Mobil, and Sunoco? Those were just a few of the thirty-five companies descended from Standard Oil.

The Standard Oil Trust branched out into many areas, and in the early 1900s, the United States government worked towards breaking the trust, which had monopolized several industries. In 1908, Benjamin O. Flower, editor of *The Arena*, offered this description:

"The Standard Oil system has extended its tentacles around the great arteries of trade and travel. Not only have the master spirits of this great trust acquired large interests in the various railway lines, but they have also acquired large interests in various local transportation companies, in electric lighting and gas companies, navigation corporations, coal and copper mines, and a number of the great banks and trust companies.

"Nor have they stopped here. Tobacco, pulp and paper corporations, fiber companies, glucose works, clock corporations, engine companies, the Steel Trust, the Western Union Telegraph Company, insurance companies, and other great interests are today represented, on their governing boards or boards of directors, by this great trust.

"More than fifty public utility corporations have directors in the Standard Oil Corporation, or brothers or sons of the master directors represented on their boards of directors. While, besides the great National City Bank of New York, known as the Standard Oil Bank, the Standard Oil interests are represented on the boards of directors of various other great banks, trust companies and insurance companies."

Flower called Standard Oil "a mighty oligarchy of privileged wealth that assumes

William Rockefeller

the attitude toward the people and the government of supreme insolence and defiance; a community of lawless wealth. Few people dream of the extent or sinister import of the Standard Oil's ramifications."

Explaining how the company wielded its power, Flower continued: "It is the greatest aggregation of capital and interests that was ever brought under one control. Transportation companies, railroads extending from the Atlantic to the Pacific and from Canada to the Gulf of Mexico; the great steel corporation, which now controls the output of iron and steel of the country; copper companies that control the production and fix the price of all our copper; companies that control the production and price of tobacco and its products.

"More than this, it controls the deposits of the great national banks and trust companies, and has taken from the savings banks, particularly those of New England, the savings of the people and has put into the banks, in place of those savings, pieces of paper called certificates of stock of these corporations.

"But greatest of all in the contest is the control it has over the weapons that must be used, the Western Union Telegraph Company and the associated press. With these it can instantly place before the people its falsehoods and slanders and keep repeating them with little or no opportunity for the other side to be heard and the facts known."

At the top of it all sat William Rockefeller. He was on the board of directors of six banks, one trust company, and at least 33 other companies. Standard Oil executives, including his son, William G., served on a variety of boards as well, granting William incredible influence over hundreds of companies, something he often wielded with a heavy hand.

As Flower pointed out, Rockefeller was relentless in his pursuit of power and money, always seeking new segments of commerce to dominate. When his attention turned to copper, William didn't stop until he had engineered a complete takeover of the industry. As an example of Rockefeller's questionable business tactics, Flower details the bold, devious maneuverings used to wring profit from the Arcadian Copper Company:

"William Rockefeller and Henry H. Rogers were on the board of directors of this company. It put the stock out at a low figure, advanced it to ninety-two dollars per share, then dropped it back, doubled the capitalization, put it up to ninety dollars, and induced the public to buy it because the Standard Oil Company was behind it.

"It then turned out that there was no copper, and that all the property that the company had was a second-handed mill (located on leased land) that had been mortgaged to Albert C. Burridge, one of its directors. All the money the public lost had gone into Standard Oil."

states and from the federal government, all in relation to issues with Standard Oil. His father was the chief financial officer, assisted by William G., and in dad's absence, the son faced intense pressure from investigators.

As Henry Rogers, William G., and John D. himself were testifying in March 1906, word came that William Rockefeller had left Italy to visit Nice and Cannes in France, and that he "was in perfect health." So much for the supposed cancer, and the mysterious ailment that had prompted doctors to urge an extended vacation in the first place.

By June, the Interstate Commerce Commission ended its investigation into Standard Oil. A waiting period ensued while government officials decided what action should be taken.

Coincidentally, it was revealed that William Rockefeller had arrived back in the United States prior to July 10, barely a month after the hearings had ended. Still avoiding detection, he had taken the unusual route of crossing the ocean to land in Quebec, Canada, and then traveling by car through the international border crossing at Rouses Point, New York.

From there, he headed west to his Bay Pond preserve, spending at least a week in seclusion before taking the train to his Tarrytown estate. His presence in the Adirondacks had been kept secret to avoid confrontation with the hostile mountain residents who had been further riled by the arrest and conviction of Rockefeller's so-called game protectors.

While Rockefeller's travels were making headlines, the turmoil across the northern region had continued unabated for months. The appellate court's pending ruling on Oliver's case was sure to have a tremendous impact on the lives of mountain residents, and the future of the mountains themselves.

Willard Saunders knew this, and he prepared meticulously for his presentation to the high court. A great deal was at stake, and he attacked each of a dozen issues vigorously. Two of the arguments appeared to hold particular promise.

Regarding Rockefeller's claim to control of the waters of the St. Regis by virtue of his land ownership, Saunders noted: "The Middle Branch of the St. Regis River neither rose nor emptied nor ended on plaintiff's alleged private park. It ran across it.

Plaintiff did not own this stream, nor did he own more than a parcel of land about and underneath it."

The argument had further merit. Just as a man could purchase land on both sides of a road but could not block the public from driving on it, Rockefeller should not be allowed to block New York State's citizens from fishing in a public stream that crossed land he had purchased.

Another strong contention of Saunders dealt with the public highway issue that had been raised across the Adirondacks: "The defendant traveled and fished on the highways and roads thereon only. The evidence shows that the roads used by defendant have been physically defined and apparent on plaintiff's land and in constant and uninterrupted use by the public for more than thirty years. They were public highways."

Finally, in November 1906, the defining moment arrived. The court battle between Rockefeller and Lamora ended nearly five years after it had begun when New York State's highest court affirmed the judgment of the lower courts. Oliver Lamora was guilty of trespassing. He would pay the earlier fine of eighteen cents, along with $790.31 in court costs.

It was over. The ruling affected everyone in the Adirondacks. There were no clauses allowing for the pursuit of publicly funded game or fish. There were no clauses limiting land ownership in the public park to five hundred, five thousand, or even five million acres. There were no clauses allowing the use of former public highways, including rivers.

The dream of a vast public park was over. Megawealth entitled individual owners to close off huge tracts of land from the public. The argument was often advanced that the wealthy owners were protecting the land.

It echoed the reasons for a similar episode across the ocean at about the same time, when the famed site of England's Stonehenge had been unexpectedly purchased by a private owner, and then fenced off from the public.

The move prompted outrage and anger, but the new owner said he was merely protecting the historic site. Like the Adirondacks, Stonehenge was recognized as a public treasure. Unlike the Adirondacks, though, measures were taken to purchase Stonehenge and make it available once again to everyone. Not so with New York's northern mountains.

In America, the power of big money reigned supreme. An expansive mountain estate was nothing more than a display of great wealth. Hunters and fishermen in the Adirondacks knew that there was no way for a Rockefeller, a Whitney, a Webb, or anyone for that matter, to use 52,000 acres.

No man *needed* that much land, and the wealthy owners certainly wouldn't cover that much territory in a lifetime. Worse yet was the fact that they only visited their estates for relatively brief periods of time. For most of each year, no one was able to enjoy the forests owned by America's aristocrats, and locals were forbidden to enter under threat of arrest by hired guards.

In any case, even a few hundred acres would have served the needs quite nicely for a magnificent estate and game preserve. But the desire for grandiose displays of wealth and power was paramount, and there would be hell to pay for anyone who dared get in the way. Just ask the people of Brandon.

The final ruling of the court had many effects, not the least of which fell heavily upon the worn shoulders of sixty-two year old Oliver Lamora. He still owned his Brandon home, but for how long? On a Civil War pension of $8 per month, how would he come up with nearly $800 to cover court costs? It may as well have been a million.

The old man was devastated. Perhaps those who had offered financial support for his cause would help pay the price for his loss. But if no one came forward, and he now stood alone, Lamora might have to surrender his home to help meet the great debt imposed by the court.

For poor Oliver, there was no rest. Three days after the ruling against him, he was back in court on the illegal venison charges from fifteen months earlier.

The timing was suspicious, of course. More than a year to prepare a case involving, at most, three witnesses? It was the Rockefeller way in all endeavors: always moving forward, always on the attack.

But now it had descended to the level of a personal vendetta. He would do his best to destroy Oliver Lamora. And in the past,

Rockefeller's best had always been more than enough.

Jury selection proved to be a difficult process, especially in light of the fact that the nearly five-year Rockefeller-Lamora case had just finished. There were many who still sympathized with Lamora's position, and certainly no shortage of citizens who were decidedly against the concept of private parks. As one newspaper put it, "several visitors at the court were sworn in for jury duty."

This would be a difficult case to defend. A deer carcass had been found in a pork barrel in Oliver's basement in the month of August. The law specifically forbade such possession. One newspaper said Lamora argued that "the meat was left at his house, but he did not know it was venison. The jury disagreed."

The case remained unsettled due to a dispute over legal proceedings, and was rescheduled for the Supreme Court docket in early 1907. In April, a second trial was held, resulting in yet another harsh blow for Oliver.

He was found guilty by the jury, and a fine of $100 was assessed, sinking him ever deeper into the financial abyss. The fine was more than his war pension for an entire year.

Meanwhile, the fortune of his court adversary, William Rockefeller, had recently been assessed at around $200 million, while son William G. stood at around $75 million. In the financial stratosphere was John D., whose worth was gauged somewhere in excess of $500 million. Neither Lamora nor anyone else had much of a chance against such wealth and power.

But America wasn't built on people who feared another's size or strength, and Oliver Lamora was nothing if not genuine pioneer stock.

Legally, he had won many battles, but lost the war. Morally, nearly everyone agreed with Lamora's position. From simple farmers to newspaper editors, men of principle knew that what Rockefeller and others had done was wrong, but legal. It was wrong for America to decide issues based solely on income. It just didn't seem to fit with "all men are created equal."

For Oliver, it was a very difficult time. Most of his friends had been driven from Brandon in the past five years. The early mass exodus had been followed by a constant trickle of departures, prompted by harassment from Rockefeller's men.

In April 1907, another Brandon property was sold. The population of the village now stood at about twenty-five die-hards, and if Oliver didn't receive help, Brandon would soon lose its most famous citizen of all.

Fortunately for Lamora, donations continued to trickle in, bolstered by the perception that he had "fought the good fight." He was one man, but he represented the interests of many. People appreciated his efforts and admired his tenacity. They demonstrated their support financially, enabling him to keep his tiny homestead.

It was clear by Rockefeller's constant efforts that he wanted Brandon removed, and especially its most caustic irritant, Oliver Lamora. But in spite of the difficulties that might lie ahead by staying in Brandon, the retired war veteran was content to live out his remaining years in quiet solitude. Now that he had lost his court case, there would be no more hunting, fishing, or trespassing on Rockefeller property. The long battle was over.

But for William Rockefeller, it wasn't over until he had won on *his* terms. Lamora's virtually invisible one-hundred foot square lot was a tiny, festering sore amidst Rockefeller's 52,000 acres. It didn't matter that Oliver would abide by the law and no longer trespass. Rockefeller wanted him gone.

In comparing the two men, Lamora came up wanting in the usual standards of measurement, things like income, schooling, business acumen, and social status.

But Oliver was a tough, determined man who stood strong in the face of adversity, and he backed up his beliefs with action. Respect for the law is vital in a democracy, but often just as important is the concept of civil disobedience. The price for breaking the law can be costly in many ways, and Oliver had paid that price many times over.

On that warm spring day back in 1902 when he crossed Rockefeller property to go fishing, Lamora knew full well that he faced trouble ahead, as he had been previously warned to stay away. He later freely testified to those facts in court. But Oliver felt strongly that he had to face the challenge, and thus the consequences. His character would not let him walk away.

For in resilience, stubbornness, fortitude, and heart, Lamora was more than Rockefeller's equal. His spirit was indomitable.

Imagine the daunting prospects. A poor, aging woodsman, supplementing a meager pension of $8 per month with fish and game that he took regularly to ensure his survival.

Suddenly, unexpectedly, he was deprived access to the sources of food and fuel that had long provided life's necessities, and enhanced its pleasures. The reason? The preference of one man's whim over the needs, wants, and very lives of others.

The poor man had very limited options before him. He could flee, or he could stand and fight. Sizing up his opponent, William Rockefeller, he saw a man with no unfulfilled desires, a financial titan with the world's largest fortune behind him. A man who, in partnership, had subdued companies, indeed, entire industries, all run by very learned, powerful men. A corporate bully feared by politicians and businessmen alike.

And yet Oliver chose to fight.

During the five-year battle, Lamora had delivered some blows, and taken many as well. He had been knocked down, but always rose to fight again another day.

Now, was it finally over? Had Lamora, like John Melin at Tarrytown, been weakened to the point where he could no longer muster the resolve to resist? If so, it had been a courageous fight. Certainly nobody would blame Oliver if he surrendered.

That may well have been William Rockefeller's assessment of his mountain-man opponent. He had made every effort to crush Oliver's spirit, defeated him in court, and drained his finances. He could just step back now and allow the poor, broken man to realize the futility of his struggle.

But, with a strategy that could have come straight from the Rockefeller playbook, Oliver Lamora came up swinging.

It was a legal move that smacked of genius, rocketing negative headlines about William Rockefeller from coast to coast. And it all had to do with a controversial action taken by Rockefeller four years earlier, when he successfully petitioned Postmaster General Henry Payne for the closure of Brandon's post office. Here's how it all played out.

Just a few weeks after the announced closing of Brandon's

post office in summer 1904, Payne had died. Robert Wynne had been appointed to the position, and he was soon besieged with complaints about the closing of the Brandon branch.

Wynne was seen as only an emergency replacement for Payne, and was expected to hold office for several months at most. During that short period, much to the chagrin of William Rockefeller, the Brandon Post Office had been reestablished.

James Bristow, fourth assistant postmaster general, had been instrumental in restoring Brandon's post office. However, his zealous investigation into all facets of postal operations led to his reassignment in January 1905, clearing the way for more shenanigans and behind-the-scenes maneuvering within the postal department.

On March 6, 1905, just thirty-nine days after the Brandon Post Office had reopened, Robert Wynne had been replaced by George Cortelyou to serve during Roosevelt's second term.

Henry Payne had long been tied to the Rockefellers through his financial interests in several railroads. As it turns out, George Cortelyou was no stranger to the Rockefellers either. In fact, years earlier, Cortelyou had been offered a chance to go into business with the Rockefeller brothers. That offer had been communicated to Cortelyou through none other than Henry Payne, his predecessor as postmaster general.

It comes as no surprise, then, that William Rockefeller went right back to work on trying to eliminate the Brandon Post Office through Postmaster General Cortelyou. It didn't happen quickly, but with the usual Rockefeller persistence, it did happen.

On January 3, 1906, the decision was made to once again close the Brandon Post Office, effective January 31. For the second time in less than two years, the village had lost its mail service, with all functions transferred to Bay Pond.

George Cortelyou had a policy of allowing no interviews of himself or his subordinates, making it very difficult for reporters to gather any information on the change. Worse yet, there was no James Bristow in the department to set things right, and pleas for the reversal of the decision fell on deaf ears.

Disgruntled Brandonites were once again forced to trek for miles among scores of No Trespassing signs in order to receive their mail at the post office on Rockefeller's estate.

In March 1907 Cortelyou was replaced by George Meyer, a wealthy man who proved to be an unexpected star of Roosevelt's cabinet. Meyer took the business of government seriously, and offered quality advice to the president. He also instituted many changes that improved both the morale and the services of the postal department.

It was at this time, just a few months after George Meyer was sworn in as postmaster general, that Lamora struck back at William Rockefeller.

After all the court battles, Oliver had been convicted of trespassing, and the restrictive injunction secured by Rockefeller four years earlier was still in place. It had once been a slap at Lamora, but now he turned it against Rockefeller.

The plan was brilliant in its simplicity. Oliver pointed out that the narrow terms of the injunction prohibited him from entering William Rockefeller's land for any reason. Thus, he was unable to visit Bay Pond's post office to receive his monthly government pension for service in the Civil War.

Oliver took his story to the newspapers, and soon Postmaster General Meyer's office was besieged by complaints from far and wide against William Rockefeller.

One letter decried the practice of allowing "a post office on the grounds of a millionaire, depriving people of their rights and cheating them of their liberties." A man from the Panama Canal Zone said Rockefeller's action "was an outrage."

War veterans fired off angry letters of protest against the treatment of one of their own. One eloquent citizen from Iowa offered this view:

> The establishment of a post office in Rockefeller's grounds, which no one can enter except by special favor of the proprietor, is peculiar and disgraceful, and a stench in the nostrils of all who love righteousness and the square deal.

Just as effective was the barrage of headlines that graced the front pages of most major newspapers once they picked up the story, including the *New York Times* and *The Washington*

Post. Some led with "Old Soldier Oppressed by Oil King" and "Veteran Soldier Barred by William Rockefeller." Others said "Aged Pensioner Persecuted by Rockefeller" and "Post Office Department to Examine William Rockefeller's Spite Work."

None of the stories were complimentary in the least to Rockefeller, and some were downright humiliating. Many noted that, though he may have done nothing illegal, Rockefeller had clearly violated the laws of human decency.

Any semblance of ethics had been cast aside in favor of avarice, and to satisfy a grudge. In effect, those were the same comments that were circulating about the Standard Oil Trust.

Standard Oil didn't *need* to control the nation's railroads or mines, just as William Rockefeller didn't *need* 52,000 acres of Adirondack land. Both Standard Oil and William Rockefeller were already incredibly wealthy by any measure. Something else, be it greed, or power, was the driving force behind the virtual obsession with more, more, more.

Most of what Rockefeller did certainly appeared to be legal, but then again, laws aren't passed by the poor. And no laws were in place to limit the power of companies that had swelled to unforeseen proportions. Soon that problem would be addressed, and the Standard Oil Trust would be dismantled after having grown beyond the scope and power of current laws.

But as yet there was no litmus test, no established standard, regarding personal fortunes. In America, you could disrupt people's lives, destroy them financially, or crush them with legal action, as long as you could afford it.

Yes, most of what Rockefeller did to the people of Brandon and to Oliver Lamora was within the law. Some editorials suggested that if what he and others had done wasn't illegal, then perhaps it should be.

The anti-Rockefeller headlines generated by Lamora's post office story spread far and wide to every corner of the nation, and in newspapers of all sizes. This was big news. For the past several decades, no one could recall a company or an individual standing up successfully to the intimidating power of the Rockefellers.

Sure, some had resisted, but in the end, the Standard Oil behemoth and the fortune it had generated had always come

Aerial view of Bay Pond

Aerial view of Bay Pond

out on top.

But now, Oliver Lamora had struck a blow for the little man. As word began to spread, the snowball effect took over. The deluge of letters to the Post Office Department demanded action, with the suggestion that the Brandon Post Office be reestablished. Postmaster General Meyer promised to examine the issues and seek a solution that would prove more convenient for the people of Brandon.

Meyer would not serve as a Rockefeller tool. He had restored the integrity of the department and did not want a return to the scandals of the recent past. He made a thorough and expeditious review of the entire case, and immediately dispatched an inspector to the Adirondacks to obtain a firsthand, in-depth assessment of the situation.

Barely a week after the torrent of negative headlines about Rockefeller had begun, Meyer announced his decision. Brandon would once again have its post office.

Lamora was ecstatic. He had beaten Rockefeller at his own game. A lesser man might have been cowed by the odds against him, or demoralized by earlier defeats. But Oliver stood tall for what he believed in. He refused to be dismissed by William Rockefeller or any other man.

The victory gave a boost to the spirits of those who had hung tough at Brandon, and it relieved them of the annoyance of the highly inconvenient mail trips they had endured for so long. It didn't change their prospects for growth as a village, but with their own post office, at least they were still on the map.

The defeat was a considerable setback in Rockefeller's effort to dispose of Brandon. With the loss of the battle over the post office, he would have to regroup and come up with a new angle. His past indicated that another attack was sure to come at some point. Brandonites knew it was important to stay alert.

In the wake of Oliver's success, the war of words and the controversy surrounding private parks continued to dominate the media in northern New York. Lost in the hubbub was the fact that the man selected as Brandon's new postmaster, Ludger Grenier, eventually declined the appointment.

Grenier had previously agreed to accept the position,

but adjacent to his name in the official government Record of Appointments is one simple entry on July 15, 1907: "pm declines." No further explanation was given, either privately by Grenier or publicly in the government register. There is no record of postal service at Brandon from that time on.

In December 1907, several months after the postal uproar subsided, a story broke that initially gave great hope to the anti-private-park faction. From Chateaugay to Lowville to Albany, it was reported that William Rockefeller had finally surrendered.

This was spectacular news. The item was picked up by the wire services and appeared in newspapers as far away as Iowa, Texas, and California.

Adirondack trappers were cited as the source of claims that the Rockefeller preserve was no longer guarded. It was said that the public now roamed freely on the rich man's estate, with no worry of harassment. This startling, wonderful change was attributed to the resistance mustered by locals during the past several years.

The only problem was that the story wasn't true. The hoax appeared to have originated in Saranac Lake, and when William Rockefeller became aware of it, he and Superintendent John Redwood issued a statement in January 1908, countering the story. They made it clear that all poachers and trespassers would be prosecuted with the same intensity as had past violators.

The more radical element of the anti-Rockefeller crowd soon put the claim to the test, keeping Attorney John Kellas busy in court prosecuting locals on a variety of trespassing charges and hunting violations.

The resourceful sportsmen of the north had little in the way of resistance to combat the hunting ban, since Rockefeller owned nearly the entire forest around Brandon. They did, however, find a way around the prohibition against fishing.

Outside of a few lots in Brandon village, virtually the only property not owned outright by Rockefeller was the railroad tracks of the New York & Ottawa. That line had once belonged to John Hurd, but had gone into receivership when Hurd's business failed.

In early 1905, the line had finally been taken over by the

New York Central, and William Rockefeller was placed on the board of directors. Though he had a controlling interest in the railroad, he didn't actually own the line itself.

Enterprising individuals recognized this loophole and had taken to walking the path of the rails to where they crossed the St. Regis River. In this way, Oliver and the other fishermen were able to access some of the best trout fishing in the north, regaining a pleasurable pastime and a valuable source of food for their survival.

William Rockefeller would have none of it. In an outrageous display of greed and vindictiveness, he leased the right-of-way of the entire 150 miles of New York & Ottawa tracks. Where the rails passed through the Brandon area, he ordered his guards to post notices that the land was now controlled by Rockefeller, and that all trespassers would be prosecuted. Eventually, the entire line was similarly posted.

Clearly, it wasn't *what* they were doing that riled him so much as *who* was doing it. For years, Rockefeller had shared the waters of his estate with his wealthy friends, and frequently issued fishing permits to business associates and acquaintances

Enterprising Brandon fishermen used this railroad bridge site south of the village to legally access the St. Regis River. When Rockefeller learned of this, he purchased the right-of-way from the railroad and banned all anglers from the river.

from area towns.

The Flanagan brothers from the famed Hotel Flanagan in Malone made many such trips, usually accompanied by other well-to-do members of society, including doctors, lawyers, and politicians. Local dignitaries from Franklin and St. Lawrence counties were granted access, but people of lesser means were excluded.

It was also known that Rockefeller, his family members, and their guests seldom fished the waters of the St. Regis. They had camps at several locations on ponds across the estate, and that's where they did most of their fishing and hunting.

Even though locals were using legal railway access to fish the largely unused river, Rockefeller simply didn't want them there. They were not breaking any fishing or trespassing laws and were not interfering with anyone. The purchase of the right-of-way and closing of the land was an aggressive act by Rockefeller, driven by nothing but spite and selfishness.

At times it really was a wonder that Rockefeller had not met the same fate as Orrando Dexter. He had, in fact, taken many steps to ensure against it. His actions had created many enemies and generated plenty of hatred, so he had taken to arriving unannounced at his estate, and retained many armed guards. Both facts were crucial to his continued well-being.

By this time, the village of Brandon had been rendered nearly extinct from the nine-year assault by Rockefeller. Oliver Lamora's house was one of only four left occupied. The population numbered between twenty and twenty-five inhabitants, all living in the oppressive shadow of the great preserve. They could do little except use the train station to gain access to other villages, where they could seek work and purchase the goods they needed for daily survival.

The summer of 1908 was an unusually dry season. As fall arrived, the extreme conditions continued, and soon the mountains were ablaze with dozens of forest fires. The central Adirondacks were hardest hit, while smaller, scattered fires struck locations in Franklin County.

The fire nearest to Brandon was located in the vicinity of Owl's Head, some twenty miles northeast. But suddenly, reports came in of a fire on the Rockefeller estate. As employees battled the inferno, new fires were reported at other locations across the preserve.

Despite the tinder-dry conditions, the forest bordering Rockefeller's estate remained intact even as the preserve woodlands were consumed by flames. His men became suspicious of the origin and location of so many fires. State officials at Albany were notified, and an investigation was launched.

In the meantime, Rockefeller's property burned while the owner seethed, envisioning a repeat of 1903, when 40,000 acres of his estate had been scorched, much of it intentionally set ablaze by disgruntled locals.

In all, forest fires consumed more than 170,000 acres of Adirondack timber in 1908. By the end of October, the state's investigation of the Bay Pond fires was completed, and officials offered the results in a brief, telling announcement:

> Several of the recent forest fires on the preserve of William Rockefeller in Franklin County were set by persons believed to have a grievance against the well known resident of New York. Mr. Rockefeller sustained considerable loss as a result of these fires.

It was uncertain whether the arson was the work of those most affected by Rockefeller's recent purchase and posting of the railroad right-of-way. By then he had acquired so many enemies that officials were unable to pinpoint the source of the fires.

Whatever the case, the beauty of his estate was once again badly diminished.

8

Steadfast to the End

In comparison to the previous seven years, 1909 was a relatively quiet period in the struggle between Rockefeller and Lamora, at least publicly. There was subtle maneuvering on several fronts as Rockefeller tried yet again to negotiate a deal to move the railroad that ran through Bay Pond and Brandon.

He also had his attorneys at work trying to effect a settlement on behalf of his estate superintendent, John Redwood, and gamekeeper Harry Melville. The appeal of their convictions on charges of keeping dogs illegally and hounding deer still had not been heard. Remarkably, no action had been taken on the case for more than three years.

Finally, in January 1910, Redwood had his day in court. He may have held some sway by virtue of his past service as a deputy sheriff and his current position as supervisor for the town of Brandon. Still, the charges against him were brought by John Burnham, a highly respected state official.

Burnham had spent a week tracking Redwood and Melville through the Brandon estate in 1906, and had offered testimony detailing the illegal actions of the hunters.

But all of that may not have mattered, as Rockefeller and his attorneys had been hard at work behind the scenes. When the case was finally heard, the defense claimed that Redwood and Melville had simply been fox hunting with a dog tethered on a chain and under their full control.

This appeared to be in clear violation of Part II, Article VI, Section 79 of the Forest, Fish, and Game Law, which said, in part:

> Dogs shall not be permitted by the owner, or persons harboring the same, to run at large in or to be taken into forests inhabited by deer or kept or possessed in the Adirondack Park.

Inexplicably, the jury quickly accepted the fox-hunting explanation by the defense, rendering a verdict of "no cause for action." In effect, it said that Burnham had brought a frivolous lawsuit. It was a stunning, incomprehensible decision.

State Attorney Hamilton Ward Jr. was highly skeptical of the jury's conclusion. There was a strong suspicion that something was amiss. Three years earlier, he had obtained a conviction on the same charges, and had been threatened by Rockefeller's attorneys at the end of the trial.

The reversal, and the unexplained three-year delay, were perplexing, to say the least.

Historically, no matter what his opponent was doing, Rockefeller remained on the attack. It came as no surprise that Redwood's acquittal was followed quickly by another broadside against Lamora.

Barely a week after Redwood's court appearance, Oliver's son, William, aged thirty-six, was arrested based on information provided by Rockefeller employees.

Depositions by Douglas Smith and Guy Chanter of the Bay Pond estate stated that Fred McNeil had been hunting at night and had killed a deer at Follensby Junior Pond. Smith and Chanter claimed that McNeil had been accompanied by William Lamora.

(Like Oliver, McNeil was already persona non grata at Bay Pond. If you recall, it was McNeil who reported having walked all the trails of the preserve in 1904 for the eighteenth consecutive year, in hopes the information would help Lamora's original court case against Rockefeller.)

The charges by Smith and Chanter against Lamora were placed on January 21, but the alleged violation had occurred on September 20 of the previous year. (The 1909 deer season ran from September 16 to October 31.) Why the four-month delay in reporting the violation?

Fred McNeil was the person accused of shooting the deer, but he had not been arrested or even questioned during the past four months. McNeil had since gone to Florida, a place he had been visiting regularly for more than a decade.

It was only after he left on the latest trip that Smith and Chanter had come forward with their accusation. The timing of the charges was clearly suspicious.

William Lamora was accused of having been in the company of McNeil when the alleged crime took place. The official charge was complicity in the illegal killing of a deer, but no deer carcass was produced as evidence.

The accusation was based solely on the word of two Rockefeller employees who, apparently struck by a belated sense of civic duty, felt compelled to report a crime they had witnessed four months earlier.

In those days, if a defendant hadn't actually pulled the trigger, a case like that against William Lamora generally was tossed out by any judge. It happened repeatedly in courts across the region.

But with William Rockefeller involved, this was no ordinary case, and the charges stood, despite the fact that there was no supporting evidence other than the statements by Rockefeller's employees.

William Lamora pleaded not guilty, and a trial by jury was set for January 31, only ten days later. This was in sharp contrast to the four-month delay in filing the complicity charges against him, and the three-year gap between John Redwood's court appearances.

Public outcry was immediate and bitter. It was widely believed that these were trumped-up charges, another vengeful form of harassment by William Rockefeller. Many claimed the accusation was bogus, an idea concocted to gain revenge on

Fred McNeil, and to strike once again at Oliver Lamora.

Why would Rockefeller want revenge on McNeil? It was Fred McNeil who had been the informant for Burnham in the conviction of John Redwood, Rockefeller's top man. Ten days after Redwood's subsequent appeal and acquittal, two of Rockefeller's men brought the delayed charges against McNeil and Lamora. Another remarkable coincidence.

Poor William Lamora had little chance in the case. He was ill-equipped to defend himself, having suffered from brain fever as a young child, which caused a degree of mental disability. In many respects, he was a child in a man's body.

His only potential defense witness was McNeil, who was in Florida, and was still unaware that charges had been placed. William prepared as best he could to do battle with Rockefeller's attorney, John Kellas, but Oliver knew his son would face a difficult time on the witness stand. Kellas was a tough litigator, and though William was a grown man, he lacked the reasoning capacity of most adults.

Though soon to be sixty-six years old, Oliver had plenty of fight left in him. But, by now, his finances were badly depleted, and attorney's fees were certain to add to his debt. He believed that a jury trial would result in an acquittal, but Oliver did not want to put his son at the mercy of Rockefeller's attorney.

And, should he somehow lose, the penalty included a fine, plus court costs. On the other hand, a guilty plea would likely involve little expense other than the court-imposed fine. In most cases, a minimal charge like that against William was settled with a penalty of a few dollars.

The risk was too great. Though William wanted to battle on, Oliver convinced him to enter a guilty plea. The show was over before it had even begun. The jury members and Rockefeller's group of witnesses were dismissed by the court.

Spectators at the Saranac Lake courthouse were shocked when Justice Seaver A. Miller imposed the maximum fine of $25 for the single violation. A reporter later noted that "Lamora Sr. broke down and wept in court after paying the fine."

That moment confirmed for many what the Brandon mainstays had known all along. For all his money and power,

William Rockefeller knew little of humanity and compassion. He would do anything to win, no matter what the cost to others.

Measures he had taken against innocent civilians were at times callous, mean-spirited, and hateful. Whether he was dealing with people or with other companies, power and control were of the utmost importance.

Sadly, for Oliver Lamora and the people of Brandon, there was never the possibility of live-and-let-live. It was not the Rockefeller way. They hadn't known it from the start, but they knew it now.

For Oliver, a fighter all his life, it was difficult to accept the defeat. He had never chosen the path of least resistance, but there were other issues at stake, and other people who would have suffered from the fight. He simply did what he felt was best and then went home to Brandon.

The fact that Oliver could still go home to Brandon remained a major irritant for Rockefeller. He had begun purchasing village properties nine years earlier. Only four homes remained occupied in the village, but for Rockefeller, that was four homes too many.

In typical Rockefeller fashion, William had been plotting another attack even while preparing for the trial of Lamora's son. This scheme involved taking advantage of business and political connections to remove Brandon's train station.

It was a goal that he had worked towards on many other occasions, but it had proven difficult to accomplish. Now, the situation appeared ripe for the possibility.

Due to its dwindling population, Brandon had for many years been reduced to a flag stop, where trains passed by unless a flag or a lantern indicated there was business at the station.

So few outsiders had been using the railroad to Brandon that in late 1906, when Paul Smith's Electric Railway line was completed from the hotel south to Lake Clear Junction, stagecoach service connecting Smith's hotel to Brandon had been abandoned.

From then on, visitors to Paul Smith's and the Saranac Lakes area could no longer access the region from the rails north of Brandon. Smith's electric railroad was making five trips per day to Lake Clear, rendering the twenty-year-old northern access route obsolete.

The combined reduction in stage and rail service added impetus to Rockefeller's assault on Brandon. Employing a new strategy, he now planned to eliminate the train station altogether by using his leverage in the railroad industry.

Exercising his influence, Rockefeller dispatched Albert H. Harris, vice-president and general counsel of the New York Central Railroad, to speak on his behalf. It was the New York Central that controlled the New York & Ottawa line running through Bay Pond.

Harris was sent before the Public Service Commission to plead the case for the abandonment of Brandon's station. He began by citing the greatly reduced rail traffic as one factor to consider, due largely to the severely diminished populations of both Brandon and Derrick.

Another argument that carried much weight was the expectation for eventual removal of the line, since Rockefeller already owned most of the property in that section, and he preferred to see the tracks completely torn up. It was pointed out that this would also help reduce the number of fires blamed on the railroads each year.

But, if that were to be done, the commission wondered, what would become of the people of Brandon? Granted, there were only twenty or so residents still living there. But the train provided the only clearly legal access to the outside world, since Rockefeller claimed to own the highways in all directions.

Harris had an answer at the ready. William Rockefeller had offered a magnanimous gesture to the people of Brandon. He would allow them to use a marked access road across his property so they could reach the rail depot at Bay Pond, some three miles to the southeast.

Henceforth, they could use that train station until a decision was made about abandoning the entire line. After all, their mail was already delivered to Bay Pond on a daily basis. It sounded indeed like the citizens of Brandon would be well taken care of, thanks in no small part to good neighbor Rockefeller.

Rockefeller's plan seemed at once both flawless and helpful, and Harris delivered it with eloquence and conviction. There was only one factor that Harris and Rockefeller had failed to take into account: Oliver Lamora.

While Rockefeller was exerting his influence and calling in favors, Lamora hadn't been sitting idle. He made an appeal directly to the Public Service Commission, alerting members to the details of Brandon's recent struggles. He petitioned strongly for the station to remain.

He noted that Rockefeller claimed ownership of all egress points from the village, and had leased the railroad right-of-way so that residents could not even set foot upon the path followed by the tracks. They already had to cross Rockefeller property just to reach Brandon's own station within the village, and did not wish to be forced into any further trespassing situations.

If they were to use the nearest available outlets, Madawaska was four miles north, and Bay Pond was more than three miles south. The distance to either destination would impose a real hardship on the citizens of Brandon.

Plus, both routes involved traveling on Rockefeller's private roads and being confronted with hundreds of No Trespassing signs.

On Rockefeller's behalf, Harris countered by citing some very compelling numbers. Brandon passenger traffic for the past year had a total dollar value of only $454.84, while freight traffic had generated a miniscule $41.84 in the past ten months. How, then, could the commission justify maintaining the station?

Fully confident of victory, Rockefeller ordered the Brandon train station torn down in anticipation of the commission's announcement, further inconveniencing local residents. When waiting to flag down the train, they now even lacked protection from the weather.

In April 1910, the Public Service Commission announced their decision. The application for abandonment of Brandon Station was denied. Oliver had done it again.

With no money and no political influence, he had defeated William Rockefeller. Disheartened by his son's recent court appearance, Oliver had somehow risen from the depths of despair to score a remarkable victory.

It was truly amazing. Twice now Lamora had beaten one of the world's most powerful, influential men, a financial titan who had never lost in the public arena, no matter who the adversary.

The commission's ruling shocked Rockefeller and brought to an end any hope of removing rail service to Brandon until the village was completely abandoned.

Though the Public Service Commission's ruling hinged on several factors, there was a single overriding consideration, well-articulated by one report in particular:

> It is not believed to be good public policy that people desiring to reach a railroad should be obliged to travel over a private road, especially when that road bristles with notices forbidding trespassing.
>
> The fact that Mr. Rockefeller is willing to allow this private road to be used at the present time for access to the station cuts no figure in the matter, and the public should not be dependent upon any man's favor in obtaining access to a public utility.

Locally, Oliver was hailed as a hero. For eight years he had battled William Rockefeller, faced with seemingly impossible odds. It is hard to imagine a more one-sided contest, but he met harassment and intimidation with courage and fortitude. Against one of the country's most powerful, richest men, Oliver Lamora had proven himself a formidable opponent.

Assailed by unscrupulous, unethical, and possibly even illegal tactics, the average man might have buckled. But through it all, Oliver had remained resolute.

From the very start, he had claimed to be using public highways to access public fishing streams to catch publicly raised fish. He claimed the right to hunt game that had been raised with public monies.

The running battle ranged from fishing and hunting rights to the legality of private parks, and the rights of citizens to mail and rail service. It became a fight for the survival of a village, and the right of a man to live free from prosecution and persecution.

There had never been any criminal intent, or intent to do harm. Oliver Lamora was simply fighting to defend a principle and a way of life.

In the face of withering attacks rooted in great wealth and power, he resisted defiantly. It was a task not for the faint of heart. But if Lamora had one thing going for him, it was heart.

A few weeks after the commission's announcement, Oliver was still basking in the glory of his victory. A visit to Tupper Lake was described in the *Tupper Lake Herald* and other newspapers:

> Oliver Lamora, the "Mayor of Brandon," whose name has been in print probably as much as any other man in northern New York, was in town Tuesday. Mr. Lamora very proudly showed a copy of the public service order in which the New York & Ottawa line is refused permission to discontinue the flag station at Brandon.
>
> Mr. Lamora informed *The Herald* that an effort would be made to compel the NY&O to build a station building to replace the one torn down. It is evident that the NY&O people did not anticipate that their application to close the station would be refused, and it would have been wiser if they had waited for a decision before tearing down the old station.

Oliver enjoyed support far and wide, since his clashes with Rockefeller had been featured in newspapers everywhere. Most of all, his base support in the Adirondacks was solid. He was not one of those scofflaws who continued to trespass and take game illegally just for the sake of poaching.

Even during Oliver's many court cases, dozens of poachers were arrested and fined for their actions. But Oliver handled the situation differently. He knew that such tactics ignored the overall issues relating to the past and the future of the Adirondacks. That is why he was perceived by many as having fought a good, clean fight with the best of intentions.

After nearly a decade of battling, it appeared that Oliver's war was over. The private park law was still the subject of much controversy elsewhere in the Adirondacks. For Oliver, that part of his crusade had not ended as he had hoped.

However, the subsequent assault on the village of Brandon and on his own property was uncalled for, in his estimation. Oliver never gave up, and at the end of the long struggle, he was still standing. Now, as much as possible, he hoped to settle into a quiet life in Brandon, free from harassment.

Bay Pond always seemed to be in some type of turmoil, though, ever since Rockefeller had moved into the area. The hot summer months of 1910 would be no different. By July, several weeks of very dry weather across the region threatened to spawn another season of destructive forest fires.

Of three smaller mountain fires burning early in the month, only one was reported in the northern Adirondacks. That fire was on Rockefeller's Bay Pond preserve. Officials stated they believed that particular fire was caused by sparks from a New York & Ottawa train.

The state-mandated transition to oil-fired locomotives in the Adirondacks had already begun, but had not yet reached the north. Once the change was made, a drastic reduction in the number of train-related forest fires was expected. But it appeared that the change hadn't come soon enough to spare the Rockefeller property.

For a time, the blame for that initial fire remained directed towards the train. No one wanted to mention the possibility of arson, since it might incite others to join in. Hatred against William Rockefeller was so strong that it didn't take much to bring people to action, legal or illegal.

The Bay Pond estate was already frequently targeted by poachers. For Rockefeller's most rabid enemies, a forest fire presented an opportunity for further revenge.

At this most inopportune time came another catalyst for action: the death of Henry Dexter, the father of Adirondack murder victim Orrando Dexter.

Nearly seven years had passed since his son's death, but Henry had never stopped pursuing the identity of the killer. Just a few days before he died at age ninety-eight, Dexter claimed he had obtained a positive clue in the case, though it had not been revealed.

At the moment of his death, he was said to have directed his daughter to keep up the hunt for her brother's murderer.

Henry Dexter left a standing reward of $10,000 for the capture of the killer, and notices to that effect were frequently posted in Adirondack newspapers, encouraging locals to help bring the murderer to justice.

One unfortunate effect of Dexter's exhortation to his daughter was the renewed incitement of mountain folks' anger against private parks in general, and William Rockefeller's in particular. This was attributed, in part, to the fact that Orrando Dexter and William Rockefeller had treated people in a very similar, unfriendly manner.

With Dexter gone, Rockefeller became the focus of local hatred, though it must be said he did nothing to discourage the strong feelings that were directed towards him.

Word spread that Henry Dexter's will had provided standing reward money, and soon the mountain firebugs retaliated by adding to

REWARD $10,000

—

ON SEPT. 19, 1903, MY SON, ORRANDO PERRY DEXTER, WAS FOULLY MURDERED ON HIS ESTATE IN THE ADIRONDACKS. I WISH TO PUBLISH TO THE WORLD THE FACT THAT THERE IS A STANDING REWARD OF $10,000 OFFERED BY ME FOR INFORMATION LEADING TO THE CONVICTION OF THE MURDERER; AND I HAVE IN A CODICIL TO MY WILL DIRECTED THAT SUCH REWARD BE PAID UPON THE CONVICTION OF THE MURDERER DURING THE LIFETIME OF MY EXECUTORS. INFORMATION TO BE LODGED WITH MY ATTORNEY, LEMUEL SKIDMORE, ESQ., 69 WALL STREET, NEW YORK CITY

HENRY DEXTER

SEPTEMBER 17, 1908

Replica of Henry Dexter's reward offer

the current fire's toll. The assault on Rockefeller's property was intense, and the arsonists seemed bent on destroying the entire estate.

One fire set at night on the border of the preserve burned more than five hundred acres of woodlands. State officials feared a repeat of the disastrous fire season of 1903, and more recently of 1908. The situation at Bay Pond was quickly getting out of hand. A decision was made at the state level to send in a force of guards to end the arson attacks.

An excerpt from an article in *The Constitution* of Atlanta, Georgia, offered this account:

> Attempts to destroy William Rockefeller's vast estate in the Adirondacks near Bay Pond in Franklin County, news of which had been suppressed until today, have caused State Superintendent of Forests Pettis to double the number of fire patrolmen who guard the territory from fires.
>
> The estate is now protected by at least a hundred men because of the fear that the mountaineers will carry out their threats of revenge against Rockefeller for closing up the ancient trails that lead through his lands.

It was further reported that a former military officer was put in charge of the force, and with time, the crew was able to prevent any more fires from being started on the preserve. It was remarkable that Rockefeller inspired such sustained anger that people felt compelled to strike back with hard-core, radical tactics, carrying the battle on year after year.

During the troubled times of 1910, the state was conducting a multi-tiered investigation into the practices and procedures followed by the forest commission in recent years. Among other things, there had been many complaints that wealthy individuals were allowed to ignore the law and operate at will, while the common man was frequently charged and convicted of game law violations.

Of particular interest to those in the northern Adirondacks was the case of John Redwood, Rockefeller's superintendent.

Attorney Hamilton Ward Jr. of the State Forest Commission was questioned at length about the matter.

It was recounted that Redwood and another Rockefeller employee had been charged and convicted of hounding deer, and fined $100 each.

Redwood had appealed the decision at the county level, where the jury had found "no cause for action." It was revealed that the second trial was held three-and-one-half years after the first court session, and by no coincidence, that second trial was held when the original complainant, Fred McNeil, was in Florida. With no witness available for the prosecution, the jury dismissed the charges.

The state also made the case that it was highly suspicious and unethical that Rockefeller's attorney was handling the defense of Redwood against McNeil's charges, while at the same time prosecuting McNeil on supposed game law violations attested to by Rockefeller's own preserve keepers.

Ward further testified that when Redwood had been convicted at the first trial, both he and Chief Game Protector John Burnham had been threatened by Rockefeller's attorneys, who "boasted openly that they [Ward and Burnham] would not continue a year in office. Feeling ran very high, and the trial was frequently interrupted."

When such blatant arrogance against the state attorney was revealed, taking place right in a court of law, doubters began to give credence to the stories of dirty tactics, pressure, and threats that Brandon residents claimed they faced when Rockefeller's men intimidated them into selling their properties.

That strategy had served the Rockefeller brothers well as they built a historic financial empire. Hundreds of businessmen had much to lose, and many lost it to the Rockefellers. But in the Adirondacks, the same strategy suffered in effectiveness.

In the mountains, Rockefeller was battling people who were self-sufficient, close to the land, and lived a simple life. Where a company and its executives could be quickly run out of business, it took time to wear down people who lived a basic life of survival.

They had little to lose, but knew the value of protecting

what was theirs. Most lived by a code of peaceful coexistence, not a popular credo in the life of William Rockefeller.

When Rockefeller had arrived in Brandon in 1898, the village was in rapid decline. He hired many locals to develop his estate, so the relationship started out as beneficial. When things didn't go his way regarding property purchases, people at first tolerated his reaction, but soon a resistance movement developed. Civility and respect might have gone a long way in avoiding all the trouble.

But William Rockefeller had chosen his path, marked by intimidation, threats, and No Trespassing signs. He backed Oliver Lamora and the mountain residents into a corner, and though he might eventually win, his new-found enemies made him pay dearly.

It was now eleven years since Rockefeller's first land purchase in the Bay Pond area. What was the status of his woodland kingdom, the jewel of the northern forests?

The beautiful buildings at Bay Pond were intact, but were protected by a force of armed guards. Rockefeller and his family visited in the summertime and during hunting season, but dared venture nowhere without gun-wielding bodyguards.

The great expanse of more than 52,000 acres had been ravaged repeatedly by fires, most of them set by a local population burning with animosity. In 1903 alone, 40,000 acres were left charred.

In an effort to halt the depredation by poachers, Rockefeller had resorted to cutting a fifteen-foot wide swath around his entire property, lined with warnings of prosecution for trespass. Guards in pairs, armed with rifles, patrolled the path both day and night, sometimes being fired upon by the rich man's enemies.

A number of stationary sentinels were posted, while others on horseback roamed the forest in search of violators. Armed escorts accompanied all fishing excursions within the preserve.

When Rockefeller wished to hunt, gamekeepers and guards first scouted the forest and determined whether or not it was safe to do so. Then, and only then, could Rockefeller "enjoy" his estate.

Instead of a lovely, peaceful nature preserve, Bay Pond at times more resembled a military command post, offering little chance for recreation.

The Mansfield (Ohio) *News* ran a story assessing Rockefeller's mountain retreat after a decade of fighting, and expenditures estimated at $2 million. A brief excerpt offers a glimpse from the outside world's view:

> They're poking fun at William Rockefeller up in the Adirondacks ... the preserve he has defended by armed men is just an elegant ruin. Said one guide, "The brutal peasantry of them parts has got good and even with Bill. They've fire-slashed his woods until you couldn't hide a wood tick in 'em. You couldn't find a deer in that preserve of his by chemical analysis."

It was not entirely accurate, of course, since there certainly was wildlife on the preserve. It was true, though, that no project ever undertaken by William Rockefeller had been in such disarray after more than a decade of work.

In spite of the struggles on the preserve, Rockefeller, as always, remained on the attack whenever possible. He now resisted Lamora's ongoing efforts to force the rebuilding of the Brandon train station that had been indiscriminately torn down before the commission had rendered its decision.

But Oliver was relentless in his efforts before the Public Service Commission, and by December, the New York Central Railroad, which owned the New York & Ottawa line, agreed to build a shelter for passengers. Brandon was officially restored to its previous status as a flag stop.

It appeared that the agreement had been reached only because the commission, at Lamora's behest, was about to order the railroad to replace the building. It was another victory for Oliver, badly riling William Rockefeller, who did not react well to the loss.

The shelter was soon built, but Rockefeller simply used the agreement to further harass the residents of Brandon. The commission began to receive complaints that trains were not stopping to pick up passengers, even when clearly signaled, as per protocol.

Passengers were left stranded at the station, and it appeared to be intentional. In the dead of winter in the northern Adirondacks, the results easily could have been fatal.

William Rockefeller would stop at nothing. He was now putting citizens' lives in danger, as evidenced by the following excerpt from a news item in the *Essex County Republican* of February 10, 1911:

> The station was opposed by Mr. Rockefeller, but the Public Service Commission decided that for the convenience of a few families in the neighborhood, railroad facilities should be provided. The Station was equipped with a flag and a lantern to be used in signaling trains.
>
> Friday [February 3] a funeral party went to Brandon, and was compelled to wait for the 9:00 p.m. train for transportation on the return to Tupper Lake. The train was signaled, and while its speed was slackened, the throttle was opened when the station was reached, and the party was astonished to see the train rush by.
>
> The would-be passengers were compelled to walk eight miles to Tupper Lake, and one of the party was exhausted before the village was reached. It is claimed that the railroad company is defying the order of the Public Service Commission.

Lamora and the residents of Brandon kept after the commission, which eventually required the trains to stop at Brandon whenever signaled. As always, William Rockefeller had made sure that even the simplest things wouldn't come easy for his enemies, even if it meant disobeying the law.

And once again, Oliver Lamora had been there to set him straight. When the bully pushed, you could count on Oliver to push back.

The battle over the railroad station was finished, and for the first summer since 1902, a quiet season passed for Oliver. For nearly a decade, he had stood up to every type of provocation

The Brandon Train Station (1921). When the station was torn down in early 1910, Oliver Lamora's efforts forced William Rockefeller and the New York Central Railroad to rebuild it.

Rockefeller could conceive, and effectively countered nearly every attack. Through it all, he showed the heart of a lion.

Now sixty-seven years old, Oliver began to consider different living arrangements. Three of his children lived in Tupper Lake, and Oliver purchased a lot in Tupper Lake Junction at the village's north end. He built a house there and moved his household goods, but retained his Brandon property.

Oliver planned to live out his last years among friends and family at Tupper Lake, but refused to part with his home in Brandon. Neither his powerful will nor his house in the tiny village in the woods would be controlled by William Rockefeller or any other man.

Shortly after building his Tupper Lake home, Oliver fell ill. He suffered from asthma, but this was something far worse. In February 1904, he had nearly succumbed to pneumonia, and now his lungs were once again badly infected. This second bout with pneumonia would be his last.

On Sunday, November 19, 1911, Oliver passed away at the home of his daughter, Lillian Farmer. The Adirondacks had lost a good one.

Had he survived just fifteen days longer, Oliver would have witnessed the resignation of William Rockefeller from his leadership position in Standard Oil. Multiple investigations into questionable business practices prompted the move.

Oliver's death marked the end of an era. There were many views on the battle between the homelanders and the wealthy newcomers. Some people expressed sympathy for the cause, and some donated money to fund the court battles.

Others held on to their own property in protest, while the more radical element trespassed, poached game, set fires, and harassed preserve guards.

But only Oliver Lamora stood in front and put it all on the line. As he testified later in court, Oliver knew on that spring day when he entered the Rockefeller preserve he faced a tough battle ahead.

Perhaps unexpectedly, after the main issue was addressed, William Rockefeller turned it into a personal battle between him and Oliver Lamora. Oliver would bend, but he would not break.

Businessmen and politicians everywhere feared William's power, and many who resisted the Rockefeller juggernaut had been crushed. Yet, a single, poor, diminutive mountain woodsman proved himself the better man.

Rockefeller may have had the world's riches at his disposal, but Oliver's courage and character had exposed his wealthy opponent for the petty, selfish bully that he was.

When Oliver died, his Brandon property still bore $401.20 of the $900 mortgage he had obtained from Willard Saunders seven years earlier. The issue of ownership remained unsettled for a time, and no one came forward to pay the outstanding debt. Eventually the property passed into the hands of Oliver's son, William, for disposal.

Two years after Oliver's death, a mortgage sale notice was posted for the required period, advising that the property would be sold at public auction on March 11, 1914. It had become perhaps the most famous one-fifth-acre lot in the country, and now there was only one interested buyer.

In late March 1914, fully twelve years after it had begun, newspaper headlines across the country trumpeted the end of the Rockefeller-Lamora feud.

The last words of the deal lacked nothing in finality: "William Lamora and wife, of Faust [Tupper Lake], to William Rockefeller of New York, property situated in the town of Santa Clara. Consideration nominal."

A reporter for the *Lake Placid News* waxed poetic on the momentous occasion:

> "To William Rockefeller, property in Santa Clara," is the last chapter in one of the most interesting and picturesque stories ever lived or written.
>
> When Mr. Rockefeller began buying land for his immense Adirondack preserve, he found no difficulties in the way of acquisition until he reached Oliver Lamora, who refused to sell his tract. Mr. Lamora was a Grand Army veteran and a woodsman, trapper, fisherman, and guide. He was contented where he was and he found no reason why he shouldn't remain.
>
> Mr. Rockefeller, however, saw otherwise. He had bought all around Oliver Lamora's tiny parcel, and he wanted that. Also, he intended to have it, and a battle followed which aroused nationwide attention.
>
> Every known means to oust a landowner was tried, but without effect on the offender, who maintained the right of a man in a free country to make and keep his home where he chooses.
>
> And when the sociological history of the country to cover this period is written, and tyranny in its twentieth century phases out, Oliver Lamora will stand large as the man who defied one of the money kings of the world in defense of the rights of man to his domain, and who won out and lived and died in his own beloved little home in the forest.

Within weeks after Rockefeller purchased the Lamora property, he embarked on an extensive building spree at Bay Pond. A new main camp was planned at an estimated cost of between $50,000 and $100,000. But, by late in the year, the structure's planned dimensions had ballooned to massive proportions. Instead of two stories, it was now three-and-one-half stories tall, with a projected cost of about $150,000.

The building was to be T-shaped, with both the top and the stem of the T measuring 250 feet in length and 50 feet wide. The stem of the T would feature 37 rooms for guides and servants, while the main section was intended as winter quarters for the Rockefeller family.

For safety, those inside would be protected by 180 thick plate-glass windows, perhaps allowing Rockefeller to dispense with some of the ubiquitous armed guards.

For another eight years, the Rockefeller family shared the preserve. Then, on a summer day in 1922, just a week after spending time at Bay Pond, William fell seriously ill at his Tarrytown home. Finally, like Lamora, his famous adversary, Rockefeller succumbed to pneumonia.

Shortly after he died at the age of 81, William Rockefeller's personal fortune was assessed at just over $102 million. The Bay Pond estate, employing 150 workers, was recorded as 51,810 acres, with an appraisal of $500,000. For some inexplicable reason, the official valuation just one year later was only $333,000. It certainly helped to lower the tax bill.

William Rockefeller at age sixty-six (1907)

It was also revealed that William still owned the Debar Mountain tract consisting of 12,850 additional acres. In total, he owned 64,660 acres, having sold the Everton site years earlier. What was considered the Bay Pond camp proper, with numerous buildings, covered 150 acres along the shore.

His son, William G., had long been targeted as the likeliest heir to the family fortune, but the elder Rockefeller stipulated that his resources be divided equally among his six children.

It was expected that William G. would maintain the family compound at Bay Pond, but just five months after his father died, William G. also passed away.

Within a year, the entire preserve was sold to a firm known as Bay Pond, Incorporated, Forest Products. Plans were made for continuous logging of the preserve grounds. Employees were needed, but the events of the past two decades had left no settlements nearby to provide a work force.

This called for immediate action. Plans were drawn up for many quality homes, an office building, stores, and a railroad station. The location? North of Bay Pond, near the site of the old hamlet of Brandon.

William Rockefeller had spent fifteen years dismantling the entire village, and now, less than a year after his death, Brandon was making something of a comeback. The new incarnation within a mile of old Brandon village would be known as McDonald Station.

Actually, the settlement at Brandon hadn't been entirely abandoned after Oliver Lamora's death. Black Joe Peryea and his family never left, remaining on their property until Joe passed away in 1941.

Even more remarkable than the expansion plans of 1924 were developments a decade later. In December 1935 it was announced by the forestry company that 23,013 acres of the property comprising the spectacular site at Bay Pond had been sold.

The buyer? None other than William Avery Rockefeller, son of William G., and grandson of William, the Standard Oil titan.

Small world.

Bibliography

Adams, Samuel Hopkins. "William Rockefeller: Maker of Wilderness." *Collier's*, April 22, 1905.

The Adirondack Forests in Danger. *Manufacturer and Builder*, Volume 20, Issue 4, April 1888.

Collins, Geraldine. "Brandon, Ghost Town of Franklin County." *Franklin Historical Review, Vols. 6-10*, New York, Teach Services, 2006, pp. 26-33.

Collins, Geraldine. "John Hurd's Railroad." *Franklin Historical Review, Vols. 6-10*, New York, Teach Services, 2006, pp. 34-38.

Donaldson, Alfred L. *A History of the Adirondacks Vol. II*, (Reprint of 1921 edition published by Century Press, New York), Fleischmann's, New York, Purple Mountain Press, LTD, 2002.

Edmondson, Brad (for the New York State Archives), Environmental Affairs in New York State: An Overview, http://www.archives.nysed.gov/a/researchroom/rr_env_hist.shtml.

Hurd, Duane Hamilton. *History of Clinton and Franklin Cos.* New York, Reprint of the 1880 edition published by J.W. Lewis, Philadelphia. Produced by the Publishing Center for Cultural Resources, New York City, 1978, pp.449-450.

Jacoby, Karl. *Crimes Against Nature – Squatters, Poachers, Thieves, and the Hidden History of American Conservation*, Berkeley and Los Angeles, California, University of California Press, 2001.

Lamoureux, Michel. Quebec City, Quebec, Canada. Genealogy of the Lamoureux Family.

National Archives and Records Administration, Northeast Region. *Record of Appointment of Postmasters, 1832 – September 30, 1971*, 201 Varick Street, 12th Floor, New York, N.Y.

National Archives and Records Administration, Northeast Region. *Post Office Department Reports of Site Locations, 1837 – 1950*, 201 Varick Street, 12th Floor, New York, N.Y.

New York State Archives Cultural Education Center Room 3043, *Civil War Service Record for Oliver Lamoura, 91st Regiment, Microfilm Roll 383*, Albany, NY 12230.

Roosevelt, Theodore, Jr., and H.D. Minot. *The Summer Birds of the Adirondacks in Franklin County*, N.Y., 1877.

Seaver, Frederick J. *Historical Sketches of Franklin County*. Albany, J.B. Lyon, 1918, pp. 534-540.

Simmons, Louis J. *Mostly Spruce and Hemlock*, Tupper Lake, N.Y., Vail-Ballou Press, 1976.

Surprenant, Neil. *Brandon: Boomtown to Nature Preserve*, Paul Smith's, N.Y., St. Regis Press, 1982.

Trimm, Mary Gerber. *History of Brandon*, Self-Published between 1993 and 2002.

William Chapman White. *Adirondack Country*, Syracuse, Syracuse University Press, 1985.

Newspaper Sources

Adirondack Daily Enterprise (Saranac Lake, N.Y.), Eddie Vogt, "Our Town." June 28, 1956.

Adirondack Daily Enterprise (Saranac Lake, N.Y.), Mrs. Albert Tyler, "This 'N That." August 20, 1956.

Adirondack Daily Enterprise (Saranac Lake, N.Y.), Eddie Vogt, "Our Town." June 28, 1956.

Adirondack Daily Enterprise (Saranac Lake, N.Y.), Mrs. Albert Tyler, "This 'N That." August 20, 1956.

Adirondack Daily Enterprise (Saranac Lake, N.Y.), "Funeral Rites Held for Fred LaMora." November 8, 1957.

Adirondack Daily Enterprise (Saranac Lake, N.Y.), "Mrs. LaMora, 84, Dies After Long Illness." March 21, 1961.

Adirondack Daily Enterprise (Saranac Lake, N.Y.), "Mrs. Lillian Farmer Dies At Tupper Lake." February 2, 1962.

Adirondack Daily Enterprise (Saranac Lake, N.Y.), "Obituaries – Charlie Farmer." November 16, 1962.

Adirondack Daily Enterprise (Saranac Lake, N.Y.), "Obituaries – Wilfred LaMora." August 28, 1972.

The Adirondack News (St. Regis Falls, N.Y.), "Brandon." March, 1887.

The Adirondack News (St. Regis Falls, N.Y.), "Local All Sorts." March 12, 1887.

The Adirondack News (St. Regis Falls, N.Y.), "Local All Sorts." May 27, 1887.

The Adirondack News (St. Regis Falls, N.Y.), "Brandon." June 8, 1887.

The Adirondack News (St. Regis Falls, N.Y.), "Local All Sorts." December 17, 1887.

The Adirondack News (St. Regis Falls, N.Y.), "Local All Sorts." January 21, 1888.

The Adirondack News (St. Regis Falls, N.Y.), "Brandon." February 26, 1888.

The Adirondack News (St. Regis Falls, N.Y.), "Keese Mills." March 24, 1888.

The Adirondack News (St. Regis Falls, N.Y.), "A Few Questions for Taxpayers to Answer." May 3, 1888.

The Adirondack News (St. Regis Falls, N.Y.), "Private Adirondack Park 200,000 Acres." May 15, 1889.

The Adirondack News (St. Regis Falls, N.Y.), "Railroads in the Adirondacks." July 12, 1889.

The Adirondack News (St. Regis Falls, N.Y.), "Extension of the N.A.R.R." November 30, 1889.

The Adirondack News (St. Regis Falls, N.Y.), "Brandon." March 26, 1890.

The Adirondack News (St. Regis Falls, N.Y.), "Change of Venue." July 5, 1890.

The Adirondack News (St. Regis Falls, N.Y.), "Court Proceedings." March 21, 1891.

The Adirondack News (St. Regis Falls, N.Y.), "Fire at Brandon." July, 1891.

The Adirondack News (St. Regis Falls, N.Y.), "Local All Sorts." September 26, 1891.

The Adirondack News (St. Regis Falls, N.Y.), "Notice of Limited Partnership." October 1, 1891.

The Adirondack News (St. Regis Falls, N.Y.), "Adirondack Pleasure Trip." October 17, 1891.

The Adirondack News (St. Regis Falls, N.Y.), "Fire at Brandon." July, 1891.

The Adirondack News (St. Regis Falls, N.Y.), "Dr. Webb Sells." July 20, 1892.

The Adirondack News (St. Regis Falls, N.Y.), "Fire at Brandon." July 30, 1892.

The Adirondack News (St. Regis Falls, N.Y.), "Local All Sorts." January 28, 1893.

The Adirondack News (St. Regis Falls, N.Y.), "Local All Sorts." February 24, 1894.

The Adirondack News (St. Regis Falls, N.Y.), "Local All Sorts." December 8, 1894.

The Adirondack News (St. Regis Falls, N.Y.), "John Hurd's Law Suit." April 6, 1895.

The Adirondack News (St. Regis Falls, N.Y.), "The N.A. Railroad Sold." June 1, 1895.

The Adirondack News (St. Regis Falls, N.Y.), "Local All Sorts." December 21, 1895.

The Adirondack News (St. Regis Falls, N.Y.), "Local All Sorts." April 24, 1897.
The Adirondack News (St. Regis Falls, N.Y.), "Local All Sorts." September 25, 1897.
The Adirondack News (St. Regis Falls, N.Y.), "New Railroad in Difficulty." October 9, 1897.
The Adirondack News (St. Regis Falls, N.Y.), "The N.Y. & Ottawa Railroad." November 6, 1897.
The Adirondack News (St. Regis Falls, N.Y.), "Local All Sorts." January 21, 1898.
The Adirondack News (St. Regis Falls, N.Y.), Untitled, Left Column. February 18, 1898.
The Adirondack News (St. Regis Falls, N.Y.), "Local All Sorts." March 12, 1898.
The Adirondack News (St. Regis Falls, N.Y.), "NY&ORR Schedule." July 30, 1898.
The Adirondack News (St. Regis Falls, N.Y.), "Miscellaneous Items." August 6, 1898.
The Adirondack News (St. Regis Falls, N.Y.), "NY&ORR Schedule." November 12, 1898.
The Adirondack News (St. Regis Falls, N.Y.), "Miscellaneous Items." December 3, 1898.
The Adirondack News (St. Regis Falls, N.Y.), "The Rockefellers' Cottage." May 13, 1899.
The Adirondack News (St. Regis Falls, N.Y.), "Miscellaneous Items." May 27, 1899.
The Adirondack News (St. Regis Falls, N.Y.), Untitled, Left Column. June 10, 1899.
The Adirondack News (St. Regis Falls, N.Y.), "Miscellaneous Items." June 24, 1899.
The Adirondack News (St. Regis Falls, N.Y.), Malone Farmer reprint. July 8, 1899.
The Adirondack News (St. Regis Falls, N.Y.), "Court Proceedings." October 14, 1899.
The Adirondack News (St. Regis Falls, N.Y.), "Miscellaneous Items." February 3, 1900.
The Adirondack News (St. Regis Falls, N.Y.), "Forestry." February 10, 1900.
The Adirondack News (St. Regis Falls, N.Y.), "Local News Items." August 19, 1900.
The Adirondack News (St. Regis Falls, N.Y.), "Local News Items." October 6, 1900.
The Adirondack News (St. Regis Falls, N.Y.), "Local News Items." December 8, 1900.
The Adirondack News (St. Regis Falls, N.Y.), "NY&ORR Schedule." October 20, 1900.
The Adirondack News (St. Regis Falls, N.Y.), "Miscellaneous Items." July 3, 1901.
The Adirondack News (St. Regis Falls, N.Y.), "NY&ORR Schedule." October 19, 1901.
The Adirondack News (St. Regis Falls, N.Y.), "Moira." March 26, 1902.
The Adirondack News (St. Regis Falls, N.Y.), "Nicholville." August 30, 1902.
The Adirondack News (St. Regis Falls, N.Y.), "NY&ORR Schedule." October 25, 1902.
The Adirondack News (St. Regis Falls, N.Y.), "Miscellaneous Items." December 22, 1902.
The Adirondack News (St. Regis Falls, N.Y.), "Local News Items." December 27, 1902.
The Adirondack News (St. Regis Falls, N.Y.), "Miscellaneous Items." March 14, 1903.
The Adirondack News (St. Regis Falls, N.Y.), "Of Local Interest." March 18, 1903.
The Adirondack News (St. Regis Falls, N.Y.), "N.Y. & O vs. Turner." May 2, 1903.
The Adirondack News (St. Regis Falls, N.Y.), "Miscellaneous Items." May 16, 1903.
The Adirondack News (St. Regis Falls, N.Y.), "NY&ORR Schedule." May 16, 1903.
The Adirondack News (St. Regis Falls, N.Y.), "Dexter Assassinated." September 26, 1903.
The Adirondack News (St. Regis Falls, N.Y.), "Lamora Wins Again." December 26, 1903.
The Adirondack News (St. Regis Falls, N.Y.), "N.Y. & Ottawa Wins Suit." February 20, 1904.
The Adirondack News (St. Regis Falls, N.Y.), "Local News Items." January 21, 1905.
The Adirondack News (St. Regis Falls, N.Y.), "Local Department." March 8, 1905.
The Adirondack News (St. Regis Falls, N.Y.), "May Change Route." September 22, 1906.
The Adirondack News (St. Regis Falls, N.Y.), "Saunders for Senator." September 29, 1906.
The Adirondack News (St. Regis Falls, N.Y.), "Reward $10,000." March 18, 1909.
The Adirondack News (St. Regis Falls, N.Y.), "Driven Out By Rockefeller." April 16, 1910.
The Adirondack News (St. Regis Falls, N.Y.), "Miscellaneous Items." December 10, 1910.
The Adirondack News (St. Regis Falls, N.Y.), "Attorney Leslie M. Saunders." Special Section, 1911.
The Adirondack News (St. Regis Falls, N.Y.), (William Rockefeller dies.) July 1, 1922.
The Adirondack Record – Elizabethtown Post (Elizabethtown, N.Y.), "Rockefeller May Purchase Forest Tract." November 14, 1935.

The Anaconda Standard (Anaconda, Montana), "The Men Who Formed the Amalgamated Plan." July 22, 1904.

The Chateaugay Record (Chateaugay, N.Y.), "Increased Customs Receipts." February 2, 1900.

The Chateaugay Record (Chateaugay, N.Y.), "Rockefeller's Home in Adirondacks Valued at $500,000." June 23, 1922.

The Chateaugay Record (Chateaugay, N.Y.), "An Adirondack Feud Recalled." October 26, 1923.

The Chateaugay Record (Chateaugay, N.Y.), "When Lamora and Rockefeller Clashed – Part 1." September 11, 1942.

The Chateaugay Record (Chateaugay, N.Y.), "When Lamora and Rockefeller Clashed – Part 2." September 18, 1942.

The Chateaugay Record and Franklin County Democrat (Chateaugay, N.Y.), "Adirondack Notes." July 19, 1901.

The Chateaugay Record and Franklin County Democrat (Chateaugay, N.Y.), "Home Matters." August 29, 1902.

The Chateaugay Record and Franklin County Democrat (Chateaugay, N.Y.), "Home Matters." May 19, 1905.

The Chateaugay Record and Franklin County Democrat (Chateaugay, N.Y.), "Home Matters." June 2, 1905.

The Chateaugay Record and Franklin County Democrat (Chateaugay, N.Y.), "Home Matters." May 26, 1905.

The Chateaugay Record and Franklin County Democrat (Chateaugay, N.Y.), "Home Matters." August 20, 1905.

The Chateaugay Record and Franklin County Democrat (Chateaugay, N.Y.), "Local Department." August 23, 1905.

The Chateaugay Record and Franklin County Democrat (Chateaugay, N.Y.), "Local Department." October 4, 1905.

The Chateaugay Record and Franklin County Democrat (Chateaugay, N.Y.), "Local Department." October 13, 1905.

The Chateaugay Record and Franklin County Democrat (Chateaugay, N.Y.), "Local Department." November 3, 1905.

The Chateaugay Record and Franklin County Democrat (Chateaugay, N.Y.), "Supreme Court Notes." November 16, 1906.

The Chateaugay Record and Franklin County Democrat (Chateaugay, N.Y.), Untitled. December 22, 1907.

The Chateaugay Record and Franklin County Democrat (Chateaugay, N.Y.), "Rockefeller Surrenders in Big Fight." January 3, 1908.

The Chateaugay Journal (Chateaugay, N.Y.), (Untitled, Column 3). July 2, 1903.

The Chateaugay Journal (Chateaugay, N.Y.), (Untitled, Column 4). July 8, 1903.

The Chateaugay Journal (Chateaugay, N.Y.), "O.P. Dexter Assassinated!" September 24, 1903.

Colorado Springs Gazette (Colorado Springs, Colorado), "Rockefeller-Lamora Feud Finally Ends – Son of Trapper and Hunter Decides to Sell Cabin and Clearing." March 31, 1914.

Commercial Advertiser (Canton, N.Y.), Untitled, Column 1. March 3, 1903.

Commercial Advertiser (Canton, N.Y.), "Northern New York." July 16, 1907.

Commercial Advertiser (Canton, N.Y.), Untitled. January 25, 1910.

Commercial Advertiser (Canton, N.Y.), "Of Local Interest." May 10, 1910.

Commercial Advertiser (Canton, N.Y.), "Looking Through A Main Street Window." June 26, 1932.

Commercial Advertiser (Canton, N.Y.), "Looking Through A Main Street Window." February 28, 1933.

Commercial Advertiser (Canton, N.Y.), "Looking Through A Main Street Window." October 31, 1944.

The Constitution (Atlanta, Georgia), "Firebugs Are Using Torch On Rockefeller Estate." July 17, 1910.

The Daily Northwestern (Oshkosh, Wisconsin), "New York Heirs To Great Wealth." April 21, 1900.

The Daily Review (Decatur, Illinois), "Rockefellers Flee To City – Feared Assassination If They Remained In Adirondacks." September 28, 1905.
The Daily Review (Decatur, Illinois), "A Bullet For A Rockefeller." May 23, 1905.

The Daily Courier (Williamsport, Pennsylvania), "Rockefeller Dying – Brother of John D. has Cancer of the Stomach." March 20, 1906.

The Daily Gazette and Bulletin (Williamsport, Pennsylvania), "Men of Millions." December 6, 1904.

The Daily Northwestern (Oshkosh, Wisconsin), "Family Flees From Danger." September 28, 1903.

The Decatur Review (Decatur, Illinois), "Rockefeller Against People." October 26, 1904.

Elizabethtown Post (Elizabethtown, N.Y.), "County and Vicinity." March 29, 1906.
Elizabethtown Post (Elizabethtown, N.Y.), "Convicted of Deer Hounding." May 17, 1906.
Elizabethtown Post (Elizabethtown, N.Y.), "Local and Vicinity." July 21, 1910.

The Essex County Republican (Keeseville, N.Y.), "Arrested For Being With A Man Who Killed A Deer." January 28, 1910.
The Essex County Republican (Keeseville, N.Y.), "Commission Defied." February 10, 1911.
The Essex County Republican (Keeseville, N.Y.), "Lumberjack Sky Pilot Gives Ad'k Mission History." July 6, 1945.

The Evening Telegraph (Elyria, Ohio), "Veteran Soldier Barred By William Rockefeller." July 6, 1907.

The Evening Times (Cumberland, Maryland), "People of Prominence." September 28, 1905.
The Evening Times (Cumberland, Maryland), "Veteran Fights Rockefeller – Soldier Would Not Sell." July 6, 1907.

The Evening Herald (Montpelier, Indiana), "Will Look Into It – Postoffice Department May Check Wm. Rockefeller's Spite Work." July 8, 1907.

The Evening Herald (Syracuse, N.Y.), "Court Decides Test Case." December 17, 1903.

The Fairbanks Daily Times (Fairbanks, Alaska), "How Men of Wealth Get Rid of Fortunes." October 5, 1906.

The Fitchburg Daily Sentinel (Fitchburg, Massachusetts), "Standard Control." September 24, 1907.

The Fort Wayne Journal Gazette (Fort Wayne, Indiana), "Bristow's Report Sustains Tulloch's Charges of Postal Frauds and Hits Payne." June 18, 1903.
The Fort Wayne Journal Gazette (Fort Wayne, Indiana), "Explains A Murder." September 21, 1903.
The Fort Wayne Journal Gazette (Fort Wayne, Indiana), "Unlimited Sums To Trace Murderer – Killed In The Adirondacks." September 21, 1903.
The Fort Wayne Journal Gazette (Fort Wayne, Indiana), "War of Giants – Rockefeller and Morgan Battle With Millions." November 3, 1903.
The Fort Wayne Journal Gazette (Fort Wayne, Indiana), "Murderers Lurk In The Shadows – Ready To Assassinate Rockefeller When He Visits His Country Estate." May 23, 1905.
The Fort Wayne Journal Gazette (Fort Wayne, Indiana), "Oil King Hungry For More Land." September 17, 1905.

The Fort Wayne Journal Gazette (Fort Wayne, Indiana), "Nature Sacred To Millionaires is Decreed – Rockefeller Wins and Court Bars to Public Vast Adirondack Park." November 14, 1906.
The Fort Wayne Journal Gazette (Fort Wayne, Indiana), "May Call William Rockefeller to Tell of Loan." October 10, 1907.
The Fort Wayne Journal Gazette (Fort Wayne, Indiana), "John Dee Wins Victory Over An Obdurate Landowner." April 15, 1908.

The Fort Wayne News (Fort Wayne, Indiana), "Deer Parks of Millionaire Sportsmen." November 8, 1899.

Franklin Gazette (Malone, N.Y.), "Laws of New York." April, 1879.
Franklin Gazette (Malone, N.Y.), "President Cleveland in the Adirondacks." May 30, 1887.
Franklin Gazette (Malone, N.Y.), "Brandon." December 23, 1887.
Franklin Gazette (Malone, N.Y.), "Brandon." January 13, 1888.
Franklin Gazette (Malone, N.Y.), "Local All Sorts." March 2, 1888.
Franklin Gazette (Malone, N.Y.), "A Fair View of the Question." October 19, 1888.
Franklin Gazette (Malone, N.Y.), "Local All Sorts." November 22, 1889.
Franklin Gazette (Malone, N.Y.), "News From the Summer Resorts in the Adirondack Mountains." August 12, 1898.

The Galveston Daily News (New York City, N.Y.), "One Man Against Sixty – Rockefeller's War On Brandon Has Moved Another Notch." October 26, 1904.
The Galveston Daily News (New York City, N.Y.), "Rockefeller Loses – Guards At Camp Withdrawn." December 29, 1907.

The Gazette (Malone, N.Y.), "Local All Sorts." December 12, 1890.
The Gazette (Malone, N.Y.), "Local All Sorts." December 4, 1891.
The Gazette (Malone, N.Y.), "From a Former Republican." October, 1896.

The Grand Rapids Tribune (Grand Rapids, Wisconsin), "John D. Resigns – Majority of Officers and Director Sever Connection." December 12, 1911.

Herald-Recorder (Potsdam, N.Y.), Untitled. July 19, 1907.

Indiana Evening Gazette (Indiana, Pennsylvania), "Veteran Finds Friend – Old Soldier, Repressed by Oil King, May Obtain Relief." July 9, 1907.

The Journal and Republican (Lowville, N.Y.), "Rockefeller Beaten – A Test Case Relative to Fishing in Parks and Private Preserves." December 24, 1903.
The Journal and Republican (Lowville, N.Y.), Untitled. August 9, 1906.
The Journal and Republican (Lowville, N.Y.), "His Life Threatened." August 9, 1906.
The Journal and Republican (Lowville, N.Y.), "Victim of Persecution." May 2, 1907.
The Journal and Republican (Lowville, N.Y.), "Rockefeller's Post Office." July 18, 1907.
The Journal and Republican (Lowville, N.Y.), "Rockefeller Capitulates." January 16, 1908.
The Journal and Republican (Lowville, N.Y.), "To Prevent Trespass." April 30, 1908.
The Journal and Republican (Lowville, N.Y.), "Brandon Station Remains." April 28, 1910.

Lake Placid News (Lake Placid, N.Y.), "Oliver Lamora's Land Rockefeller's At Last – Son Sells Little Homestead Made Famous By Father's Refusal To Sell To Millionaire." April 3, 1914.
Lake Placid News (Lake Placid, N.Y.), "Adirondack Battles Were Front-Page News In Those Days." August 12, 1927.
Lake Placid News (Lake Placid, N.Y.), "Bay Pond Tract in Rockefeller Family Again – Close Deal for 23,013 Acres for $225,000." December 22, 1935.

Bibliography

Lake Placid News (Lake Placid, N.Y.), "Old Joe Dies At Home Near Rocky's." June 13, 1941.

The Lincoln Daily Star (Lincoln, Nebraska), "Wealth Triumphs in Legal Battle." March 30, 1914.

The Malone Farmer (Malone, N.Y.), Untitled. January, 1900.
The Malone Farmer (Malone, N.Y.), "Railroads in the Adirondacks." January 17, 1900.
The Malone Farmer (Malone, N.Y.), "Home Matters." May 30, 1900.
The Malone Farmer (Malone, N.Y.), "Of Local Interest." June 6, 1900.
The Malone Farmer (Malone, N.Y.), "Railroad Speculations." June 20, 1900.
The Malone Farmer (Malone, N.Y.), "Home Matters." June 27, 1900.
The Malone Farmer (Malone, N.Y.), "N.Y. & Ottawa Railroad Schedule." June 28, 1900.
The Malone Farmer (Malone, N.Y.), "State Tax Sale." September 1, 1900.
The Malone Farmer (Malone, N.Y.), "Home Matters." December 5, 1900.
The Malone Farmer (Malone, N.Y.), "Of Local Interest." February 20, 1901.
The Malone Farmer (Malone, N.Y.), "News Notes." July 17, 1901.
The Malone Farmer (Malone, N.Y.), "Of Local Interest." July 21, 1901.
The Malone Farmer (Malone, N.Y.), "Of Local Interest." July 24, 1901.
The Malone Farmer (Malone, N.Y.), "News Notes." August, 1901.
The Malone Farmer (Malone, N.Y.), "Moira." March 26, 1902.
The Malone Farmer (Malone, N.Y.), "Home Matters." May 7, 1902.
The Malone Farmer (Malone, N.Y.), "Popularity Of Camp Life In The Adirondacks." May 1, 1902.
The Malone Farmer (Malone, N.Y.), "Of Local Interest." June, 1902.
The Malone Farmer (Malone, N.Y.), "Of Local Interest." August 20, 1902.
The Malone Farmer (Malone, N.Y.), "Home Matters." August 27, 1902.
The Malone Farmer (Malone, N.Y.), "Of Local Interest." September 3, 1902.
The Malone Farmer (Malone, N.Y.), "Home Matters." September 17, 1902.
The Malone Farmer (Malone, N.Y.), "Big Summer Hotels." September 24, 1902.
The Malone Farmer (Malone, N.Y.), "County Court Cases." December 10, 1902.
The Malone Farmer (Malone, N.Y.), "Court Cases." December 24, 1902.
The Malone Farmer (Malone, N.Y.), "Of Local Interest." March 11, 1903.
The Malone Farmer (Malone, N.Y.), "Forest Fires." May 27, 1903.
The Malone Farmer (Malone, N.Y.), "Forest Fires Raged Again." June 10, 1903.
The Malone Farmer (Malone, N.Y.), "Of Local Interest." July 8, 1903.
The Malone Farmer (Malone, N.Y.), "Park Rights Sustained." July 15, 1903.
The Malone Farmer (Malone, N.Y.), "Home Matters." July 26, 1903.
The Malone Farmer (Malone, N.Y.), "Of Local Interest." August 5, 1903.
The Malone Farmer (Malone, N.Y.), "Home Matters." August 12, 1903.
The Malone Farmer (Malone, N.Y.), "Of Local Interest." September 23, 1903.
The Malone Farmer (Malone, N.Y.), "On The Murderer's Track." September 30, 1903.
The Malone Farmer (Malone, N.Y.), "The Wheels of Justice." October 7, 1903.
The Malone Farmer (Malone, N.Y.), "The Dexter Case." October 7, 1903.
The Malone Farmer (Malone, N.Y.), "County Court Proceedings." December 16, 1903.
The Malone Farmer (Malone, N.Y.), "Lamora Again Wins." December 23, 1903.
The Malone Farmer (Malone, N.Y.), "Of Local Interest." March 2, 1904.
The Malone Farmer (Malone, N.Y.), Untitled, Column 3. May 25, 1904.
The Malone Farmer (Malone, N.Y.), "Local Department." August 11, 1904.
The Malone Farmer (Malone, N.Y.), "Local Department." August 31, 1904.
The Malone Farmer (Malone, N.Y.), "Local Department." September 21, 1904.
The Malone Farmer (Malone, N.Y.), "Local Department." October 12, 1904.
The Malone Farmer (Malone, N.Y.), "Local Department." October 19, 1904.
The Malone Farmer (Malone, N.Y.), "Local Department." November 9, 1904.
The Malone Farmer (Malone, N.Y.), "Local Department." November 16, 1904.

The Malone Farmer (Malone, N.Y.), "Of Local Interest." November 23, 1904.
The Malone Farmer (Malone, N.Y.), "Local Department." November 30, 1904.
The Malone Farmer (Malone, N.Y.), "County Court." December 21, 1904.
The Malone Farmer (Malone, N.Y.), "Local Department." February 22, 1905.
The Malone Farmer (Malone, N.Y.), "Local Department." May 24, 1905.
The Malone Farmer (Malone, N.Y.), "Local Department." May 31, 1905.
The Malone Farmer (Malone, N.Y.), "Local Department." August 9, 1905.
The Malone Farmer (Malone, N.Y.), "Local Department." November 1, 1905.
The Malone Farmer (Malone, N.Y.), "State Tax Sale." December 13, 1905.
The Malone Farmer (Malone, N.Y.), "Local Department." January 17, 1906.
The Malone Farmer (Malone, N.Y.), "Local Department." February 21, 1906.
The Malone Farmer (Malone, N.Y.), "Local Department." March 28, 1906.
The Malone Farmer (Malone, N.Y.), "Local Department." May 30, 1906.
The Malone Farmer (Malone, N.Y.), Untitled. June 6, 1906.
The Malone Farmer (Malone, N.Y.), Untitled. August 1, 1906.
The Malone Farmer (Malone, N.Y.), Untitled. November 21, 1906.
The Malone Farmer (Malone, N.Y.), "Supreme Court." November 21, 1906.
The Malone Farmer (Malone, N.Y.), "Local Department." March 6, 1907.
The Malone Farmer (Malone, N.Y.), "Supreme Court." April 10, 1907.
The Malone Farmer (Malone, N.Y.), "Local Department." July 10, 1907.
The Malone Farmer (Malone, N.Y.), "Local Department." January 8, 1908.
The Malone Farmer (Malone, N.Y.), "Home Matters." February 25, 1908.
The Malone Farmer (Malone, N.Y.), "Local Department." May 13, 1908.
The Malone Farmer (Malone, N.Y.), "Local Department." November 18, 1908.
The Malone Farmer (Malone, N.Y.), "Local Department." April 20, 1910.
The Malone Farmer (Malone, N.Y.), "Local Department." August 31, 1910.
The Malone Farmer (Malone, N.Y.), "Private Park." July 13, 1911.
The Malone Farmer (Malone, N.Y.), "Local Department." November 20, 1911.
The Malone Farmer (Malone, N.Y.), "Private Park." June 12, 1912.
The Malone Farmer (Malone, N.Y.), "Mortgage Sale." December 10, 1913.
The Malone Farmer (Malone, N.Y.), "Local Sidelights." April 1, 1914.
The Malone Farmer (Malone, N.Y.), "Local Department." November 25, 1914.
The Malone Farmer (Malone, N.Y.), "Local Department." August, 1923.
The Malone Farmer (Malone, N.Y.), "Local Department." October 17, 1923.
The Malone Farmer (Malone, N.Y.), Untitled. April 2, 1924.
The Malone Farmer (Malone, N.Y.), "Activities at Bay Pond." July 11, 1924.
The Malone Farmer (Malone, N.Y.), "W.J. Saunders Passes From Life At Lake Ozonia." September 28, 1932.
The Malone Farmer (Malone, N.Y.), "Deed Filed for 23,013 Acre Tract To Rockefeller." December 24, 1935.

The Mansfield News (Mansfield, Massachusetts), "Rockefeller Is Minus His Deer." September 30, 1910.

The Marion Daily Star (Marion, Ohio), "Red Roof Spoils Oil King's View." July 25, 1908.

The Marshfield Times (Marshfield, Wisconsin), "People of Prominence." June 23, 1905.

Middletown Daily Times (Middletown, N.Y.), "His Life Threatened." May 2, 1907.

Nebraska State Journal (Lincoln, Nebraska), "Rockefellers in the Deal." October 24, 1899.

The Newark Advocate (Newark, Ohio), "Threat – That Wm. Rockefeller Will Be Next Victim of Men Who Slew O.P. Dexter." October 2, 1903.

Bibliography

The Newark Daily Advocate (Newark, Ohio), "Country For The Rich." July 17, 1896.
The Newark Daily Advocate (Newark, Ohio), "Assassination." September 26, 1903.

New Castle News (New Castle, Pennsylvania), "Dies With Son's Slayer At Large." July 12, 1910.

The News (Newport, Rhode Island), "A Rockefeller Post Office." July 6, 1907.

The New York Times (New York City, N.Y.), "News of the Clubs." January 25, 1891.
The New York Times (New York City, N.Y.), "Save The Adirondacks – A List Of Preserves In Which Some Very Good And Some Very Bad Names Appear." May 20, 1890.
The New York Times (New York City, N.Y.), "What Is Doing In Society." June 20, 1900.
The New York Times (New York City, N.Y.), "What The Adirondacks Offer." June 8, 1902.
The New York Times (New York City, N.Y.), "Prominent Persons In The Adirondacks." July 28, 1902.
The New York Times (New York City, N.Y.), "Fine Homes Displacing Real Camps in Adirondacks." May 31, 1903.
The New York Times (New York City, N.Y.), "Reward For Capture of Dexter's Slayer." September 21, 1903.
The New York Times (New York City, N.Y.), "William Rockefeller Now A Fire-Fighter." May 20, 1903.
The New York Times (New York City, N.Y.), "Forest Fires Exaggerated." June 16, 1903.
The New York Times (New York City, N.Y.), "Serious Blow To Poachers." July 3, 1903.
The New York Times (New York City, N.Y.), "Week's Doings In Adirondack Camps." September 6, 1903.
The New York Times (New York City, N.Y.), "Orlando P. Dexter Shot Dead By Hidden Enemy." September 20, 1903.
The New York Times (New York City, N.Y.), "Court Stopped Fishing." September 27, 1903.
The New York Times (New York City, N.Y.), "Rockefeller Loses His Suit." December 17, 1903.
The New York Times (New York City, N.Y.), "To Save State Forests." January 8, 1904.
The New York Times (New York City, N.Y.), "Wm. Rockefeller Wins Case." June 10, 1904.
The New York Times (New York City, N.Y.), "Pastimes At Paul Smith's." July 10, 1904.
The New York Times (New York City, N.Y.), "Advertisements." July 12, 1904.
The New York Times (New York City, N.Y.), "Fighting Wm. Rockefeller – Fisherman's Case Sent Back For A New Trial." July 25, 1904.
The New York Times (New York City, N.Y.), "In The Adirondacks, Catskills, And Other Mountain Resorts." August 14, 1904.
The New York Times (New York City, N.Y.), "The Private Park Issue – Up In The Adirondacks, It's A Political Question." September 10, 1904.
The New York Times (New York City, N.Y.), "Standard Oil May Get Northern Pacific Road." October 5, 1904.
The New York Times (New York City, N.Y.), "Fire On Rockefeller Guards – Strenuous Protests of Adirondack Natives Against Game Preserves." November 23, 1904.
The New York Times (New York City, N.Y.), "William G. Rockefeller Gets Eighteen Cents Damages." December 18, 1904.
The New York Times (New York City, N.Y.), "Decision for W. Rockefeller." December 28, 1904.

The Oakland Tribune (Oakland, California), "Fighting Fires in the Forests – Strenuous Work In Which The Rockefeller Brothers Is Engaged." May 19, 1903.
The Oakland Tribune (Oakland, California), "Fished On William Rockefeller Preserve." December 17, 1903.
The Oakland Tribune (Oakland, California), "Ten Fortunes." March 1, 1906.
The Oakland Tribune (Oakland, California), "Has a Frank Passage on Big Bandwagon." July 14, 1907.

The Ogden Standard (Ogden, Utah), "People of Prominence." October 12, 1905.
The Ogden Standard (Ogden, Utah), "Lamora Feud Ends With Sale – Son of Old Trapper at Last Sells Property to Rockefeller." March 30, 1914.

The Ogdensburg Advance and St. Lawrence Weekly Democrat (Ogdensburg, N.Y.), "City Locals." July, 1903.

The Perry Daily Chief (Perry, Iowa), "Gives Up The Fight – William Rockefeller To Let Woodsmen Hunt In Peace." February 20, 1908.

Plattsburgh Sentinel (Plattsburgh, N.Y.), "Paragrams." January 25, 1882.
Plattsburgh Sentinel (Plattsburgh, N.Y.), "Partition Suit Involving 25,000 Acres." June, 1883.
Plattsburgh Sentinel (Plattsburgh, N.Y.), "Neighboring Counties, Franklin." November, 1883.
Plattsburgh Sentinel (Plattsburgh, N.Y.), "Another Extensive Adirondack Lumbering Enterprise." April 10, 1885.
Plattsburgh Sentinel (Plattsburgh, N.Y.), "New Railroad in the Adirondacks." February 19, 1886.
Plattsburgh Sentinel (Plattsburgh, N.Y.), "Adirondack Enterprises." June, 1886.
Plattsburgh Sentinel (Plattsburgh, N.Y.), "Franklin's New Lumber Region." June, 1886.
Plattsburgh Sentinel (Plattsburgh, N.Y.), "Paragrams." July 9, 1886.
Plattsburgh Sentinel (Plattsburgh, N.Y.), "Paragrams." July 30, 1886.
Plattsburgh Sentinel (Plattsburgh, N.Y.), "The President Leaves the Adirondacks." September, 1886.
Plattsburgh Sentinel (Plattsburgh, N.Y.), "Paragrams." December 10, 1886.
Plattsburgh Sentinel (Plattsburgh, N.Y.), "Neighboring Counties, Franklin." December 23, 1886.
Plattsburgh Sentinel (Plattsburgh, N.Y.), "Paragrams." April 22, 1887.
Plattsburgh Sentinel (Plattsburgh, N.Y.), "The President's Trip to the Woods." May 27, 1887.
Plattsburgh Sentinel (Plattsburgh, N.Y.), "Paragrams." June 10, 1887.
Plattsburgh Sentinel (Plattsburgh, N.Y.), "Paragrams." July 29, 1887.
Plattsburgh Sentinel (Plattsburgh, N.Y.), "Neighboring Counties, Franklin." May 11, 1888.
Plattsburgh Sentinel (Plattsburgh, N.Y.), "Neighboring Counties, Franklin." April 19, 1889.
Plattsburgh Sentinel (Plattsburgh, N.Y.), "An Adirondack Game Park – New York Men to Secure 100,000 Acres of Adirondack Forest Land." April 18, 1890.
Plattsburgh Sentinel (Plattsburgh, N.Y.), "Dr. Webb's Adirondack Park Project." June 12, 1891.
Plattsburgh Sentinel (Plattsburgh, N.Y.), "Dr. Webb Makes More Purchases." June 26, 1891.
Plattsburgh Sentinel (Plattsburgh, N.Y.), "Adirondack Forests." December 23, 1892.
Plattsburgh Sentinel (Plattsburgh, N.Y.), "Work of the Forest Commission." December 8, 1893.
Plattsburgh Sentinel (Plattsburgh, N.Y.), "Preserve the Forests." February 22, 1895.
Plattsburgh Sentinel (Plattsburgh, N.Y.), "The Adirondack Park." January 21, 1898.
Plattsburgh Sentinel (Plattsburgh, N.Y.), "Deepen Our Canal." March 4, 1898.
Plattsburgh Sentinel (Plattsburgh, N.Y.), "Local Paragrams." May 25, 1900.
Plattsburgh Sentinel (Plattsburgh, N.Y.), "Millionaires Own Adirondacks." October 4, 1901.
Plattsburgh Sentinel (Plattsburgh, N.Y.), "Term of Supreme Court." November 22, 1901.
Plattsburgh Sentinel (Plattsburgh, N.Y.), "Preservation of Forests." September 5, 1902.
Plattsburgh Sentinel (Plattsburgh, N.Y.), "Rockefeller Park." September 5, 1902.
Plattsburgh Sentinel (Plattsburgh, N.Y.), "Rockefeller Gets $200." July 31, 1903.
Plattsburgh Sentinel (Plattsburgh, N.Y.), "Forest Preserve." January 8, 1904.
Plattsburgh Sentinel (Plattsburgh, N.Y.), "State Should Own Forests – Report of Special Committee on Adirondacks." February 26, 1904.
Plattsburgh Sentinel (Plattsburgh, N.Y.), "Local Department." November 16, 1904.
Plattsburgh Sentinel (Plattsburgh, N.Y.), Untitled, Column 5. February 1, 1907.
Plattsburgh Sentinel (Plattsburgh, N.Y.), "Lamora Wins Out Against Rockefeller." July 12, 1907.
Plattsburgh Sentinel (Plattsburgh, N.Y.), "Rich Man The Murderer." November 13, 1908.
Plattsburgh Sentinel (Plattsburgh, N.Y.), "Must Not Close Brandon Station." April 22, 1910.

Bibliography

Plattsburgh Sentinel (Plattsburgh, N.Y.), "Young Lamora Fined." April 22, 1910.

Plattsburgh Sentinel and Clinton County Farmer (Plattsburgh, N.Y.), "Forest Fires Still Raging." May 29, 1903.
Plattsburgh Sentinel and Clinton County Farmer (Plattsburgh, N.Y.), "Hunt Dexter's Slayer." September 25, 1903.
Plattsburgh Sentinel and Clinton County Farmer (Plattsburgh, N.Y.), Untitled. December 25, 1903.
Plattsburgh Sentinel and Clinton County Farmer (Plattsburgh, N.Y.), "Clue To Dexter Murder." November 11, 1904.

The Post-Standard (Syracuse, N.Y.), "Getting a Big Grip on Adirondacks Region." July 6, 1899.
The Post-Standard (Syracuse, N.Y.), "Rockefeller Has No Cause – Loses in His Case Against Oliver Lamora." December 17, 1903.
The Post-Standard (Syracuse, N.Y.), "Long Litigation Settled." June 10, 1904.
The Post-Standard (Syracuse, N.Y.), "Rockefeller is Guarding Preserve." November 14, 1904.
The Post-Standard (Syracuse, N.Y.), "Rockefeller Enriched By Eighteen Cents." December 19, 1904.
The Post-Standard (Syracuse, N.Y.), "Public Trails, Private Preserves." January 10, 1905.
The Post-Standard (Syracuse, N.Y.), "A Magnate in the North Woods." April 22, 1905.
The Post-Standard (Syracuse, N.Y.), "String of Bullets To Warn Rockefeller." May 23, 1905.
The Post-Standard (Syracuse, N.Y.), "W. Rockefeller Cancer Victim." March 20, 1906.
The Post-Standard (Syracuse, N.Y.), "W. Rockefeller Home In Auto." July 26, 1906.
The Post-Standard (Syracuse, N.Y.), "Laws of New York by Authority." June 22, 1908.
The Post-Standard (Syracuse, N.Y.), "Fires Raging in Adirondacks." September 11, 1908.
The Post-Standard (Plattsburgh, N.Y.), "Offers $10,000 For Evidence in Dexter Mystery." September 30, 1908.
The Post-Standard (Syracuse, N.Y.), "Acquittal For John Redwood." January 12, 1910.
The Post-Standard (Syracuse, N.Y.), "Adirondack Feud Stirs North Folk." January 22, 1910.
The Post-Standard (Syracuse, N.Y.), "Warns Against Fires in the North Woods." July 7, 1910.
The Post-Standard (Syracuse, N.Y.), "Easement Deal on Adirondack Land Collapses." March 20, 1998.

The Racine Weekly Journal (Racine, Wisconsin), "Rockefeller Gets Damages." November 16, 1906.

Reno Evening Gazette (Reno, Nevada), "Rockefeller Awarded Eighteen Cents Damages." November 13, 1906.

The Sioux Valley News (Correctionville, Iowa), "Rockefellers Are Doing Quite Well." October 20, 1904.

The St. Lawrence Herald (Potsdam, N.Y.), "County and Vicinity." September 17, 1897.
The St. Lawrence Herald (Potsdam, N.Y.), "St. Regis Falls." October 28, 1898.
The St. Lawrence Herald (Potsdam, N.Y.), Left Column. February 24, 1899.
The St. Lawrence Herald (Potsdam, N.Y.), Left Column. April 7, 1899.
The St. Lawrence Herald (Potsdam, N.Y.), "A Private Park." April 28, 1899.
The St. Lawrence Herald (Potsdam, N.Y.), "A Mammoth Enterprise." June 23, 1899.
The St. Lawrence Herald (Potsdam, N.Y.), "Rockefeller Adirondack Purchases." July 21, 1899.
The St. Lawrence Herald (Potsdam, N.Y.), "The Blizzards." March 9, 1900.
The St. Lawrence Herald (Potsdam, N.Y.), Dickinson Center. May 23, 1900.
The St. Lawrence Herald (Potsdam, N.Y.), "County and Vicinity." January 31, 1902.
The St. Lawrence Herald (Potsdam, N.Y.), "County and Vicinity." March 25, 1904.
The St. Lawrence Herald (Potsdam, N.Y.), "County and Vicinity." June 10, 1904.

Bibliography

The St. Lawrence Herald (Potsdam, N.Y.), "County and Vicinity." July 1, 1904.

Stevens Point Daily Journal (Stevens Point, Wisconsin), "New Aristocracy of the Adirondack Mountains." April 23, 1904.
Stevens Point Daily Journal (Stevens Point, Wisconsin), "Standard Oil on the Rack." November 24, 1906.

The Sun (Fort Covington, N.Y.), "Special Mention." July 13, 1905.
The Sun (Fort Covington, N.Y.), "Special Mention." May 24, 1906.
The Sun (Fort Covington, N.Y.), "Special Mention." May 23, 1907.
The Sun (Fort Covington, N.Y.), "Lamora To Get His Mail." July 18, 1907.

The Sunday Herald (Syracuse, N.Y.), Reprint from *Forest and Garden*, "Adirondack Railroads – They Mean Destruction to the Forests Through Which They Pass." August 18, 1889.

The Syracuse Standard (Syracuse, N.Y.), "The State Park." August 27, 1889.

The Syracuse Herald – Magazine Section (Syracuse, N.Y.), "Rockefeller, With All His Millions, Can't Make A Saloon Keeper Move." February 19, 1905.
The Syracuse Herald (Syracuse, N.Y.), "Fired the Woods - William Rockefeller the Victim of Incendiaries." October 30, 1908.
The Syracuse Herald (Syracuse, N.Y.), "Rockefeller's Mountain Feud Finally Ended." March 30, 1914.

The Syracuse Herald American (Syracuse, N.Y.), Janis Barth, "LaMoras Wed Fifty Years – Anniversary Recalls Old Feud." June 21, 1953.
The Syracuse Herald American (Syracuse, N.Y.), Janis Barth, "When the wood was all used up, so was Brandon's run of good luck." June 2, 1985.

The Syracuse Herald Journal (Syracuse, N.Y.), "State Buys Whitney Adirondack Property." December 23, 1997.

Ticonderoga Sentinel (Ticonderoga, N.Y.), "The Lamora Case Again – The Question of Private Rights in Adirondack Lands." September 22, 1904.
Ticonderoga Sentinel (Ticonderoga, N.Y.), "Rockefeller's War on a Village – He is Determined to Wipe Out the Town of Brandon." November 3, 1904.
Ticonderoga Sentinel (Ticonderoga, N.Y.), "Odds and Ends." January 2, 1908.
Ticonderoga Sentinel (Ticonderoga, N.Y.), "Brandon Station Continued." April 21, 1910.

The Trenton Times (Trenton, N.J.), "Threatens To Kill Wm. Rockefeller." May 23, 1905.
The Trenton Times (Trenton, N.J.), "President Snubs Gould, Rockefeller." August 13, 1904.
The Washington Post (Washington, D.C.), "John D.'s Gay And Almost Wicked Brother William." April 30, 1905.
The Washington Post (Washington, D.C.), "Rockefeller Threatened." May 23, 1905.
The Washington Post (Washington, D.C.), "The Little Known Heirs of Well Known Men of Millions." June 11, 1905.
The Washington Post (Washington, D.C.), "Rockefeller Wins." September 15, 1905.
The Washington Post (Washington, D.C.), "The Senate of Finance – A Handful of Men Who Rule the Business World." October 19, 1905.
The Washington Post (Washington, D.C.), "Denies Cancer Story." March 25, 1906.
The Washington Post (Washington, D.C.), "Aid For Rockefeller Foe – Postmaster General To Investigate Veteran's Complaint." July 6, 1907.

The Washington Post (Washington, D.C.), "Rockefeller Loses Fight." July 14, 1907.

The Washington Post (Washington, D.C.), "John D. Can't Buy Inn." April 15, 1908.

The Washington Post (Washington, D.C.), "Bars Many From Livelihood." April 29, 1908.

The Washington Post (Washington, D.C.), "Yields to W. Rockefeller – Son of Trapper Ends Old Feud by Selling Out to Oil King." March 31, 1914.

The Watertown Herald (Watertown, N.Y.), "The Adirondacks." January 25, 1890.

The Watertown Herald (Watertown, N.Y.), "Drifting Backward." October 18, 1890.

The Watertown Herald (Watertown, N.Y.), "Carthage." November 15, 1890.

The Watertown Herald (Watertown, N.Y.), "Carthage." January 31, 1891.

The Watertown Herald (Watertown, N.Y.), "Forest Sharks." February 25, 1893.

The Watertown Herald (Watertown, N.Y.), "Editors Assembled." July 8, 1893.

The Watertown Herald (Watertown, N.Y.), "Dr. Webb's Preserve." September 9, 1893.

The Watertown Herald (Watertown, N.Y.), "Forest Preservation." December 6, 1894.

The Watertown Herald (Watertown, N.Y.), "Adirondack Squatters Must Go." December 26, 1896.

The Watertown Herald (Watertown, N.Y.), "Governor's Message." January 8, 1898.

The Watertown Herald (Watertown, N.Y.), "Adirondack Park." June 8, 1901.

The Watertown Herald (Watertown, N.Y.), "Protect The Adirondacks." March 15, 1902.

The Watertown Herald (Watertown, N.Y.), "Preserving the Forests." August 30, 1902.

The Watertown Herald (Watertown, N.Y.), "Forest Preserve." January 9, 1904.

The Watertown Herald (Watertown, N.Y.), "Opposition To Land Grabbers." February 2, 1907.

The Watertown Herald (Watertown, N.Y.), "Tour of the Town – Stealing Forest Timber." June 22, 1907.

The Watertown Herald (Watertown, N.Y.), "Tour of the Town – Closing the Adirondacks." May 2, 1908.

The Watertown Herald (Watertown, N.Y.), "The Forest Preserve." January 8, 1910.

The Watertown Herald (Watertown, N.Y.), "Rich and Poor to be Evicted." August 27, 1910.

The Weekly News (Frederick, Maryland), "Troubled Rockefellers." May 25, 1905.

Illustration Credits

Gagne, Timothy E. Pages 20, 142, 161

Library of Congress Collection. Pages 91, 128, 164

Library of Congress Collection. Page 48. Battle of Five Forks. From original lithograph by Kurz & Allison, Art Publishers, Chicago, U.S.A., 1886.

Library of Congress, Civil War Glass Negative Collection. Page 49. Five Forks prisoners. 1865.

Library of Congress Collection. Page 50. Grand Review of the Armies. Mathew Brady, 1865.

Quenell, Gregory. Page 139. Bay Pond aerial photographs.

Index